See what others are saying about this book:

"I'm impressed with Ms. Sherwood's in-depth understanding of email issues and her clever ideas for dealing with the great gobs of email many of us get."

—Steve Dorner, original author of Eudora

"Finally! This excellent book fills a void in the how-to literature, offering simple and effective tactics for anyone overwhelmed by the daily deluge of email. This book has been a great help to us and to our clients, and it can help you too!"

—Irene Tobis, Ph.D., President, Ducks-in-a-Row™ Organizing Consultants

"If you have ever felt like your e-mail was controlling you, this book can help you take back control. Office-support workers will find it particularly useful."

—Joyce Grant, Editor, *Administrative Assistant's Update*

"Email is supposed to be a tool to help you live your life. Unfortunately, most people spend more time maintaining the tool than extracting utility from it. This book gives you quick hints to reduce the time you spend configuring, filtering, and deleting mail and more time to deal with the important messages."

—Ed Krol, author of the best-selling *The Whole Internet User's Guide and Catalog* and *The Whole Internet: The Next Generation*

"I loved the tone of the book. Sherwood's sense of humor and unintimidating writing style make this a sure winner. Its wealth of information and accessibility make it an essential read for anyone who uses email."

—Trisha Gooch, Editor, *ibizTips*, Internet Business Forum, www.ibizhome.com

"This book helps e-mail novices and experienced users learn how to use Eudora and how to make effective and efficient use of e-mail. It does so in a pleasant manner with excellent examples and screenshots."

—Andrew Starr, *e*Mailman®, www.eMailman.com

"A solid book that will help anyone overwhelmed by email learn to cope."

—Adam C. Engst, author of *Eudora for Windows and Macintosh*

"*Overcome Email Overload* gives you everything you need to know to take back control of your inbox. Corporate, school and other email system managers should make *Overcome Email Overload* required reading by their users. Highly Recommended."

—Mary Houten-Kemp, creator of *Everything Email,* www.everythingemail.com

"Don't touch your email without first reading *Overcome Email Overload.*"

—Heinz Tschabitscher, Guide for About.com's Email section, email.about.com

"Eudora's design has always been driven by our desire to make email more accessible and manageable. Sherwood intimately understands that spirit in Eudora. *Overcome Email Overload with Eudora 5* is more than an instruction manual. It is a thoughtful and entertaining guide for how readers can take advantage of Eudora to make email easier to use."

—John W. Noerenberg II, Principal Engineer, Qualcomm, Inc.
(makers of Eudora)

"I really enjoyed *Overcome Email Overload with Eudora 5* and found it to be perceptive, clearly-written and very well-organized; it has many useful and practical suggestions for dealing with this very critical area of modern business life. I consider it invaluable for all of us who are impacted by this new form of communication."

—Craig D. Wandke. Interpreter Operations Manager, Language Line Services,
www.languageline.com

"I've been an avid user of email since it was introduced, but in the past few years I've really gotten buried. Sherwood's book has been a godsend to me. I particularly appreciate her skill at setting forth the 'why' as well as the 'what.'"

—Thomas Henderson, retired Chairman & CEO of Guy F. Atkinson Company

"If you don't need more time, don't read this book. If you enjoy reading all your junk mail, you may not care for it. If you have never had trouble finding an important message, this book may not be for you."

—Russell Bridges, System Administrator

For a full list of endorsements, see:

http://www.OvercomeEmailOverload.com/eudora/quotes.html

Overcome Email Overload
with Eudora 5

OTHER BOOKS IN THIS SERIES:

Overcome Email Overload with Microsoft Outlook 2000 and Outlook 2002

COMING SOON:

Overcome Email Overload with Microsoft Outlook Express

Overcome Email Overload with Netscape Communicator

Overcome Email Overload with Eudora 5

Get Through Your Electronic Mail Faster

http://www.OvercomeEmailOverload.com

Kaitlin Duck Sherwood

World Wide Webfoot Press  *Palo Alto*

World Wide Webfoot Press, PO Box 36, Palo Alto, California USA 94302-0036
http://www.webfoot.com   *eudora@webfoot.com*

First edition 2001
Printed in the United States of America

05 04 03 02 01   9 8 7 6 5 4 3 2 1

International Standard Book Number: 0-9708851-6-4

Library of Congress Control Number: 2001092505

Cover design, including cartoon, by Kaitlin Duck Sherwood

James A. DeLaHunt,
you are quite perfect enough!
Thanks for saying yes!

Contents

Preface

When I started working on this book, I thought it would be a guide to writing more effective email. After all, *A Beginner's Guide to Effective Email*, my Web-based guide to writing better email, gets 600,000 hits per year. Hundreds of people per year send me fan email.

Much to my surprise, I found that almost nobody was interested in a book on writing email well.

The people I talked to were so overwhelmed by *incoming* messages that they had stopped caring about *writing* email well. They felt that writing well was something that helped their *readers*, not themselves. With forty, sixty, one hundred, or even three hundred messages per day, they felt unable to help themselves, let alone their readers.

I believe in giving customers what they want, so I refocused the book on how to deal with email overload. Because I have gotten a lot of email myself over the past twenty-five years, I knew something about that, too.

I was surprised, however, at how much I learned about dealing with email in the course of writing this book. I could not have done it without the help of many people.

Acknowledgments

I now understand why the Academy Awards are so long and boring. While my name might have ended up on the cover, there is no way that I could have done this without the help of numerous people.

When reading acknowledgments in the past, I had always thought that spouses were shortchanged. I'd see authors heap praise after praise upon their agents, their publishers, their editors, their advisors, their neighbor's dog, their pizza delivery person, and on and on. Then, at the very end, seemingly as an afterthought, they'd thank their spouse "for everything." Apparently, the tradition is to thank people in reverse order of importance, but I didn't know that.

So to make sure that it is very clear to everybody just how important my spouse has been, I want to call attention *first* to my husband, Jim DeLaHunt. This book would not have come into being without his support. In addition to providing financial support, reviewing the book dozens of times, helping to design the cover, co-authoring the poem on page 132 and page 253, and giving me ideas when I got stuck, he provided emotional support.

Writing is emotionally difficult for me. Especially in the early days, I could find problems in my writing all too easily. Instead of facing the problems that I had to fix in the prose, it was very easy to become distracted by the nice day outside, a magazine, a book, or even cleaning the house. Jim kept reminding me that my main priority was the book, not keeping a clean house, not reading good books, and not taking long walks. But most importantly, every time I had a crisis of confidence, he would look me in the eye and say with absolute confidence, "It's going to be a great book."

Many other people helped in many ways. For starters, this book wouldn't have happened if Steve Dorner hadn't developed Eudora while working at the Computing Services Office at the University of Illinois at Urbana-Champaign.

The libraries of Stanford University, San Jose State University, Palo Alto, Menlo Park, Redwood City, Saratoga, Santa Clara, Sunnyvale, Milpitas, and Cupertino provided useful and fascinating background information.

I regret that I can't individually list the hundreds of people who sent me questions about email since I put *A Beginner's Guide to Effective Email* on the Web. While I might have grumbled to myself about all the work it took to answer them, the questions showed me what people cared about and frequently made me scratch my head and think. This book is better because of their questions.

Katrina Knight answered some obscure questions about Eudora for Windows.

I had some valuable help with my examples. I had some questions about skydiving terminology and practices that Beth Siegel answered quickly and completely. Jeff Powell and Mia Cheong Walkowski gave examples of good and bad email usage.

Jeff Ehlers and Dave Perry gave some advice on the cover design.

I learned a number of tips from various Web sources. The Eudora-Win mailing list (http://www.listmoms.net/lists/eudora-win) and the Eudora Usenet newsgroups (comp.mail.eudora.ms-windows and comp.mail.eudora.mac) answered a lot of questions. Pete Beim's Unofficial Eudora FAQs & Links page (http://wso.williams.edu/~eudora/) has an out-of-date but still extremely useful and comprehensive set of links. Finally, Adam Engst, author of *Eudora for Windows and Macintosh: Visual QuickStart Guide*, moderates a very useful discussion at TidBITS (http://www.tidbits.com).

While this isn't an academic book, I learned a lot from academic researchers. Jean Fox Tree's work illuminated the role of speech disfluencies; Bonnie Nardi's book *A Small Matter of Programming* prompted me to provide a template rules file. Francis Heylighen and Jean-Marc Dewaele's paper *Formality of Language* corroborated some of my ideas about formality and context. (Thanks to Julia Schult for finding their paper.) *Long and Short Routes to Success in Electronically-Mediated Negotiations* by Don Moore, Terri Kurtzberg, Leigh Thompson, and Michael Morris indirectly made me realize that email is more about negotiation than persuasion.

Olle Bälter's article *Keystroke Level Analysis of Email Message Organization* showed me that having more than around twenty folders and selectively deleting old messages are time-inefficient strategies. Steve Whittaker and Candace Sidner's paper *Email Overload: Exploring Personal Information Management of Email* made me understand that people use email as a "to-do" list, an idea which has permeated my book. (Thanks to Bill Walker for pushing me into reading

Whittaker and Sidner's paper and for showing me his unpublished paper on some information management software that he wrote.) Bälter and Sidner's article on *Bifrost Inbox Organizer* confirmed that prioritizing with categories was the right thing to do.

I inflicted lousy drafts upon many people, and their feedback shaped this book into what it is now. For a while it seemed like every single reviewer found one thing that would improve the book enormously—and each person found a different thing! It was frustrating to do so many rewrites, but it has made the book far, far better.

- Brendan Kehoe, Michael Brundage, Kevin Johnson of Motorola, David Strom, Geoff Mulligan, and Linda G. Brigman reviewed the book for Addison Wesley Longman. Addison Wesley Longman didn't take the book, but they provided good feedback and treated me well.
- A number of friends and relatives reviewed my manuscript. These include (in chronological order) Miriam Blatt, Martha Grant, Diana Peterson, Scott Meyers, Nancy Capulet, Georges Harik, Chris Beekhuis, Tom Lehman, Anne Powell, Charles Bry, Marda Buchholz, Chrissy Foley Lopez, Raul Lopez, Roxanne Guilhamet Maloney, David Blitz, Neil Shapiro, Joe Shakes, Lisa Egart, Barbara Leeds, Lakiba Pittman, Wendy Phillips, Ed Krol, Betsy DeLaHunt, Greg Lassonde, Day DeLaHunt, Russell Bridges, John Ciccarelli, Jennie Savage, Mike Gobbi, Heinz Tschabitscher, Mary Houten-Kemp, Mary Wisnewski, Hyung Cheong, Tony Huff, Tom Henderson, and Barbara Noparstak.
- Frank Ritter's Introduction to Information Sciences and Technology class at Pennsylvania State University gave me numerous points to think about.
- Some complete strangers generously gave me their comments. Dan Coutts, Don Hoffman of the U.S. Navy, Arta Szathmary of Bucks County Community College, Charles Sha'ban of Talal Abu-Ghazaleh & Co. in Jordan, Marcel Damseaux from Uruguay, Linda Beal of Higher Colleges of Technology in the United Arab Emirates, Rob Kelley from Australia, John M. Gancz of the Quebec Learner's Network (Canada), Mike Swift from ISG (New York), Andrew Starr of eMailman, Adam Engst (the author), and John W. Noerenberg II of Qualcomm gave me outstanding feedback. I appreciated getting viewpoints from far outside Silicon Valley.

A few authors gave me important advice and (even more important) encouragement. Nancy Capulet (*Putting Your Heart Online*), Scott Meyers (*Effective C++* and *More Effective C++*) and Ken Lunde (*CJKV Information Processing*) helped me believe that I could make the book real.

Georges Harik provided essential support.

I want to give special thanks to my mother. In addition to being an accomplished technical writer and eagle-eyed critic, she *hates* Eudora. (She much prefers the old Unix mailer.) As I *love* Eudora, her comments were an especially useful counterpoint.

Again, I couldn't have done this without my beautiful and talented husband. I hope that someday I can support him in his pursuits half as well as he supported me in mine. Thanks, Jim—for everything.

Characters and Places

Most of the examples revolve around a character named Mabel Garcia. Mabel Garcia is entirely a creation of my imagination. Her bosses, coworkers, family, friends, company, and organizations are equally fictitious.

The only exceptions are a few friends and relatives who thought it would be fun to see their names in print. While the names might exist in the real world, the characters are entirely fictitious. The "real" Martha Boise is not a lawyer and Charlie Yzaguirre isn't an electric bagpipe repair technician. Claire Beekman is a dog. (And if Georges Harik made electric bagpipes, they would *not* explode!)

Similarly, there is a town called Hoopston in east central Illinois, USA. However, there are no universities, floss recycling companies, or electric bagpipe repair shops located there that I know of. Hoopston is a perfectly charming town, but it bears no relationship to the Hoopston in this book. I just liked the name.

CHAPTER 1

Introduction

Do you ever feel overwhelmed by email? Do you ever have to struggle to get through all of your messages between meetings? Does getting one more frivolous message ever make you angry?

It probably wasn't always this way. When you started using email, you probably only got a trickle of email messages each day. After a few months, perhaps ten messages arrived in your inbox daily. A few months after that, you changed to a different department at work and started getting thirty messages per day. And yesterday you came to work and found ten messages about the facilities shutdown, five announcements that people have changed jobs, three jokes, seven messages complaining about the new lobby furniture, four announcements of new projects, eight direct questions about some aspect of your job, two notices that a red minivan's lights are on, confirmation that the book you bought on-line has shipped, and fifty other similarly random messages.

Little by little, your trickle turned into a flood, and now you are gasping for air.

Does this sound like you? If so, cheer up—you've come to the right place. This book will save your time and perhaps your sanity. Some techniques might require a little bit of work at first, but they will be worth it over time.

If you don't get this much email, count yourself lucky—for now. This book will show you how to keep from getting overwhelmed in the future.

Who Is This Book for?

This book is for anybody using Eudora 5 who gets too much email. While you need to know a few very basic things, you do not need to be an expert on Eudora 5. This book explains all the advanced features that you need to know—and doesn't waste your time explaining every single possible thing you can do with Eudora 5.

Even if you *are* a Eudora power user, this book will still be useful. Three-quarters of the book is on email *strategies*, not which button to push or which menu to pull down. If this were a book on writing, it would be something like *Effective Business Communication*, not *Mastering WordPerfect 7.3.2 in Ten Easy Steps Unleashed*.

When there is more than one page of "buttons and menus" instruction, I give the page number of the next strategy section. This lets you easily skip over material you already know. I do assume that you are familiar with the basic operations of Eudora and:

- can send and receive email messages
- can add nicknames to your address book
- can use the Find and Search tools
- can open a message in its own window
- know what mailing lists (also called *listservs, list servers, listbots,* or *distribution lists*) are

There were a few topics that clearly some people know and others do not. To give the information some people need without boring the ones who know it already, I put a very brief discussions of mailboxes and labels in Appendix B, *Mailboxes and Labels*.

If you need a comprehensive reference manual for Eudora, you should find another book. *Eudora for Windows and Macintosh: Visual Quickstart Guide* by Adam Engst (Peachpit Press, 1999) should tell you what you need.

If you are a teacher, you will find this book suitable for classroom instruction at many levels. The language in the book is easily accessible, even for teenagers. On the other hand, its deconstructions of the medium can be jumping-off points for collegiate classroom discussions. Homework exercises are available at

`http://www.OvercomeEmailOverload.com/exercises/`

While there is material that applies to anybody, I wrote this book for people who get too much email at work. Very few people are overwhelmed by messages from their closest personal friends.

Overview of This Book

Here's a preview of what you will learn in each chapter.

This book starts by explaining *filters*—instructions that you can give to your email program to organize and prioritize your messages automatically. Chapter 2 and Chapter 3 are by far the most technical of the chapters, but also the ones that I believe are the most useful. When I started using filters, I was able to get through my email messages in half the time it took before.

- Chapter 2, *Organize and Prioritize Your Messages*, gives strategies for grouping messages, shows how to create filters, and gives strategies for showing a message's importance.
- Chapter 3, *Useful Filter Recipes*, is a "cookbook" with examples of useful filters.

Finding and selecting a message in Eudora doesn't take much time, but it's something you do over and over. A little bit of time saved on each operation can add up quickly.

- Chapter 4, *Move Around Your Messages Quickly*, shows keyboard and mouse shortcuts for navigating through your messages more efficiently.

Reading messages more efficiently helps enormously, but if you still have to read and respond to a hundreds of messages per day, it might not be enough.

- Chapter 5, *Reduce the Number of Incoming Messages*, gives strategies for reducing the number of messages you get.
- Chapter 6, *Spend Less Time on Responses*, shows how to cut down on the amount of time you spend composing replies, while still being responsive to the messages that matter.

Another way to save time is to *write* better messages. A miscommunication means more work for you—which usually means more email. Reducing your load by writing well is such an important topic that it's split into four chapters.

- Chapter 7, *Reduce Ambiguity*, shows how to make the content of your messages more clear. If you write clear messages, people won't have to send you further messages asking for an explanation.
- Chapter 8, *Convey Emotional Tone*, gives strategies the emotional tone more clear. You won't have to spend as much time explaining your intentions.
- Chapter 9, *Make Messages Legible*, shows how to send messages that your correspondents can read easily. This reduces the number of times you'll have to send a message.
- Chapter 10, *Get and Keep Attention*, shows how to improve the chances that your correspondents will notice, understand, and reply to your messages. This means less time you'll spend on getting a response or action from your correspondents.

At some point, regardless of how well you manage your own email, you'll be limited by your coworkers' email habits.

- Chapter 11, *Improve Your Company's Email Effectiveness*, discusses techniques for improving email efficiency for your whole organization.

Each chapter ends with a set of summarizing bullet points.

Appendix A has an extensive glossary. I do define almost all technical terms, abbreviations, and jargon the first time I use them, but I realize that you might not read the whole book straight through. I also don't define some of the more elementary terms. Finally, the Glossary defines some email terms that this book doesn't use, but that you might see in other places.

As mentioned earlier, Appendix B discusses mailboxes and labels.

Eudora Versions

There are many different versions of Eudora. There are Windows and Mac OS versions of all three Eudora 5 modes: Paid, Sponsored, and Light. As far as the material in this book is concerned, the three versions have very few differences. I will point differences out as they come up.

(If you are using Eudora 5 at work, you probably have Paid mode. Paid mode costs money and has all the features. Sponsored mode has all the features and is free, but you have to look at advertising. Light mode is free but doesn't have as many features as Sponsored and Paid mode.)

There are many older versions of Eudora, but fortunately Qualcomm is very good at maintaining compatibility between versions. If you use an older version, the pictures might look different, but most of the features discussed in this book are essentially the same. You can learn more about how your version's lack of features affects material discussed in this book at:

> `http://www.OvercomeEmailOverload.com/eudora/versions.html`

Additional Material

While I only have a limited amount of space in this book to cover material, the Web is not limited. There is additional material at this book's Web site:

> `http://www.OvercomeEmailOverload.com/eudora`

The site has:

- exercises for students
- visual aids (overheads) suitable for lectures
- a list of errors that were found after the book went to the printers
- template files that you can download and use
- links to sites with further information

Notation, Terminology, and Simplifications

Please take a moment to read about the notation and terminology. Understanding the notation will help you spot examples more easily and recognize how I've simplified things. Understanding the terminology will make the explanations easier to follow.

Sections that mainly cover which buttons to push and which menus to pull down have section headers that start with "How to..."

I use a `fixed-width font` for anything that the computer would print or that you would type.

If you need to select something from a menu, I use arrows (→) to show the order of the menu selection. For example, if I tell you to select `Message→New Message`, that means that you should first select the `Message` menu, then select `New Message` from the choices that appear.

I sometimes combine Mac OS and Windows commands with a slash. For example, almost all keyboard shortcuts are identical between Mac OS and Windows except for the modifier keys. I sometimes write instructions like "press `Command/Control-w` to close the window." That means that if you are using Mac OS, then you should press `Command-w`; if you are using Windows, you should press `Control-w`.

All filter recipes (covered in Chapter 2 and Chapter 3) are double boxed like this:

```
when a message arrives
if To: contains roses-talk@rosegardens.org
then Transfer To mailbox RoseGardening
```

Figures showing Eudora windows don't reproduce particularly well and have a lot of unimportant details. I therefore usually show email messages as text instead of as screen shots. Email messages have a light grey background like this:

```
Subject: This is in the header of an example message.
Date: Mon, 1 Jan 2000 20:09:59 -0800
From: sender@catfloss.org
To: receiver@catfloss.org


This is the body of an example message.
```

I need to explain some of the email terms as well. Unfortunately, the terminology of email is a bit odd.

- **Body:** The *body* is the actual text of the conversation. In the example above, the body is This is the body of an example message.
- **The header:** The information *about* a message is called the header. That's what's above the line in the example above. The header includes things like who the message is to, who it is from, when it was sent, what the subject is, and so on.
- **Headers:** Each line in *the* header is called *a* header. For example, the Subject: line is *a* header. So is the Date: line; so is the From: line. They are all *headers*. (I didn't come up with this terminology, I'm just reporting it.)

I don't show all possible headers. Email messages usually have ten to twenty headers, most of which are only interesting to email programs or the programmers who write them. These headers are so dull, in fact, that Eudora usually hides most of the headers from you.

Unless a header is important to an example, I leave it out. For example, if I am not discussing dates or times, I leave out the Date: header. I even leave out the From: and To: headers frequently.

When I show the header in an example, a thin black line separates the header and body. The header is above the line and the body is below the line.

I usually leave out email signatures in examples. Signatures are useful, but they take up space that I'd rather use for explanations.

Tips

I put short pieces of advice that don't fit in the flow of the text into TIP boxes, like this:

TIP: To see all the headers, including ones Eudora normally hides, open the message in its own window. Click on the button near the upper left corner that says BLAH BLAH BLAH.

Quotes

Eudora usually shows quotes in email messages with black vertical lines that it calls *excerpt bars*. However, people using different email programs usually see ">" at the beginning of your quoted lines, even if you see excerpt bars when you create the message. Because of that—and because it is difficult for me to simulate excerpt bars in my text layout program—I almost always show quotes with ">".

Examples

Many of this book's examples deal with personal email. I know that many companies do not allow personal email, but too many examples about database upgrade projects would bore you.

Summary

- This book is for non-technical people who have some experience with email already, use it mostly at work, and get lots of it.
- This book covers filters, navigating more efficiently, reducing the number of incoming messages, spending less time on responses, writing clearer messages, and improving your organization's email culture.
- Words in `fixed-width font` represent things that either you type or your computer displays.
- The body of a message is the actual information conveyed; the header is information about the message.
- All email messages in this book will be in a box with a grey background. If I show the header, there will be a thin black line separating the header and body.
- To save space in examples, I don't show headers and signatures unless they help clarify the example.
- In this book's examples, quotes will usually be marked with ">" at the beginning of the line instead of excerpt bars.

CHAPTER 2

Organize and Prioritize Your Messages

If you are like most people, you go through your messages in the order that they arrive. This can be very inefficient: you can spend so much time on low- or medium-priority messages that you don't get to a time-critical message until it's too late.

Perhaps you skim the subjects and guess what is important and what isn't. Unfortunately, relying on your eyes and memory can be dangerous. You might see an urgent message that distracts you enough that you forget to go back and deal with an important but less-urgent message. You might even overlook an important message completely.

Think about how you handle your paper mail. You undoubtedly sort your paper mail quickly before you read it. Having messages categorized helps you figure out what to look at first, what to read later, and what to ignore.

Prioritizing your email messages can help as much as prioritizing paper mail. If your messages are sorted into groups of related messages, then you can:

- **Match your response speed to message priority.** You can look at high-priority groups of messages often and ignore low-priority groups until you have a free moment. For example, you might want to examine messages from your closest coworkers the moment the messages arrive but wait until the end of the day to read through a company-wide announcements list.
- **Remember discussions.** If you read all the messages on a topic one after another, you are likely to remember what was in earlier messages on that topic. If a lot of unrelated messages separate two related messages, you might not understand the later message without re-reading the earlier one.

- **Judge the amount of traffic on a topic.** Grouping related messages together makes it easy to see how many new messages on a particular topic have arrived. The number of related messages can give you a clue about what action you should take. Suppose, for example, that someone sends a message that asks a question. If you see a lot of responses to that message, someone else has probably already answered the question. You will then know to read all the responses before replying, instead of composing a response right away.

Fortunately, Eudora has tools that can organize and prioritize messages for you. These tools—called *filters*—can move messages into different mailboxes based on rules that you set up. For example, you might set up your filters to file all messages from a mailing list into its own mailbox.

Setting up filters is probably the single most important step to take to regain control of your email. It does take some effort to set up filters, but it is well worth it. This chapter gives strategies for prioritizing messages, discussing how to:

- group related messages together
- configure filters in Eudora
- keep track of messages you aren't done with
- test your filters
- keep messages and their responses together
- organize with multiple accounts

This chapter is by far the most technical chapter of the whole book. But while filters might look intimidating, they aren't actually very difficult. If you can follow written directions to bake a cake or change a sparkplug, then you can set up filters.

Group by Category

You may be tempted to use filters to move messages to different mailboxes. However, when messages are spread across many mailboxes, most people have a hard time keeping track of messages that they haven't finished with yet.

In most cases it's better to prioritize by categorizing messages with labels. With labels, you can assign a category and a color to a message. To assign categories and colors to labels, select Special→Settings...→Labels (Mac OS) or

`Tools`→`Options…`→`Labels` (Windows). (For more about labels, see "Labels" on page 250.)

Assign labels to all your incoming messages, sort your inbox by label, and remove messages from your inbox when you have finished with them. This lets you see all of your "to-do" messages quickly and in priority order, as shown in Figure 1:

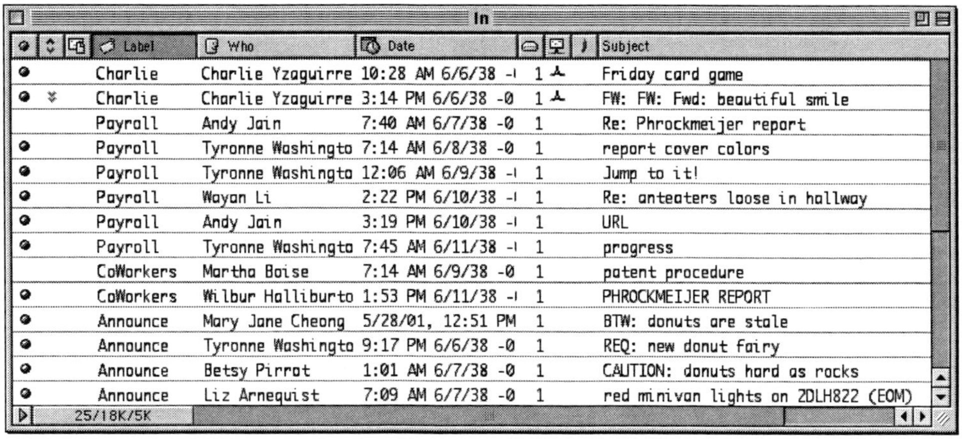

			Label	Who	Date				Subject
●			Charlie	Charlie Yzaguirre	10:28 AM 6/6/38 -1	1		⊥	Friday card game
●	⯬		Charlie	Charlie Yzaguirre	3:14 PM 6/6/38 -0	1		⊥	FW: FW: Fwd: beautiful smile
			Payroll	Andy Jain	7:40 AM 6/7/38 -0	1			Re: Phrockmeijer report
●			Payroll	Tyronne Washingto	7:14 AM 6/8/38 -0	1			report cover colors
●			Payroll	Tyronne Washingto	12:06 AM 6/9/38 -1	1			Jump to it!
●			Payroll	Wayan Li	2:22 PM 6/10/38 -1	1			Re: anteaters loose in hallway
●			Payroll	Andy Jain	3:19 PM 6/10/38 -1	1			URL
●			Payroll	Tyronne Washingto	7:45 AM 6/11/38 -1	1			progress
			CoWorkers	Martha Boise	7:14 AM 6/9/38 -0	1			patent procedure
●			CoWorkers	Wilbur Halliburto	1:53 PM 6/11/38 -1	1			PHROCKMEIJER REPORT
●			Announce	Mary Jane Cheong	5/28/01, 12:51 PM	1			BTW: donuts are stale
●			Announce	Tyronne Washingto	9:17 AM 6/6/38 -0	1			REQ: new donut fairy
●			Announce	Betsy Pirrot	1:01 AM 6/7/38 -0	1			CAUTION: donuts hard as rocks
●			Announce	Liz Arnequist	7:09 AM 6/7/38 -0	1			red minivan lights on 2DLH822 (EOM)

25/18K/5K

Figure 1: Messages Sorted by Label

The label's name is usually visible in a column towards the left side. Messages with labels `Charlie`, `Payroll`, `CoWorkers`, and `Announce` are visible in Figure 1. If your `Label` column is not visible, select `Special`→`Settings…`→`Mailbox Display` (Mac OS) or `Tools`→`Options…`→`Mailboxes` (Windows), and put a check in the box marked `Label`.

Note that when you sort a mailbox by label, it's sorted by the order of the labels in the `Special`→`Settings…`→`Labels` (Mac OS) or `Tools`→`Options…`→`Labels` (Windows) windows, not alphabetically by the name you give to the label. For example, Figure 1 shows messages with the label `Payroll` sorted before messages with the label `Announce`. You should assign your labels in order of priority.

When you sort a mailbox by label, Eudora shows messages with no labels before messages with labels. If you are using Eudora for Mac OS, messages with system labels will appear before messages with Eudora labels.

Organize Your Categories

If you are used to filing paper documents, you might want to have lots and lots of categories. However, categorizing electronic mail messages is very different from filing paper documents. Finding an old paper memo can take so long that retrieval time is much, *much* more significant than filing time. It makes sense to have lots of categories for paper. Eudora's excellent sorting and searching tools make finding old messages much faster, so filing speed is much more significant than retrieval speed. This means you don't need as many categories for your email as for your paper documents.

Giving each of your projects its own label is usually not a good idea. In addition to requiring many labels, this strategy guarantees that some email messages will be difficult to categorize. Email messages that mention two different projects could go in either project's category. Furthermore, categorizing based on project is very difficult to do automatically. Computers are still a lot dumber than humans: they don't do a good job at figuring out what a message *means*.

It is much easier to categorize based on what group the sender belongs to. There is always one and only one sender of a message, and people usually fit into relatively well-defined groups in your life. Your groups might include:

- coworkers in your immediate group
- other people in your company
- relatives
- friends
- fellow members of volunteer organizations
- various mailing lists that you've subscribed to (both work and personal)
- retailers that you have a relationship with
- retailers who are trying to get your business (junk email)
- automated response programs (such as order confirmations or account information)

TIP: It's okay if your categories have different amounts of email. The goal is not to split mail into equal piles, it's to prioritize quickly and easily.

While mailing list messages can be from many different people, I think of the messages as being "from" the mailing list. They are usually to the same address and so are easy to group together. Grouping keeps the conversations intact.

I make an exception for jokes and do not categorize by sender. Usually the sender didn't write the joke, and a joke almost never has anything to do with your relationship to the sender. Furthermore, jokes almost never need a response. If your filters can tell that a message is a joke, they should put it in a jokes-only category, regardless of who sent it.

If You Have More Categories Than Labels

Unfortunately, you probably will have more categories than labels. Eudora for Mac OS has fifteen labels, which might be enough if you don't subscribe to many mailing lists. However, Eudora for Windows only gives you seven labels to work with.

If you don't have enough labels for all of your categories, you might think of using the same label for several categories. For example, you could use one label for all of your mailing list messages. Unfortunately, that would mean that all of your mailing list messages would be mixed together.

A better strategy is to use treat categories slightly differently depending upon their priority. You will probably find that you have three types of categories:

- high-priority: with messages that might turn into "to-do" items,
- medium-priority: with informational messages that are not likely to turn into "to-do" items, and
- low-priority: with messages that you don't want to read.

Assign your labels to high-priority messages. If you don't have enough labels for your medium- and low-priority categories, group their messages together in their own mailboxes. Because the medium- and low-priority messages are not likely to turn into "to-do" items, your inbox should still have all of your important messages.

Here's an example of how someone might set up her labels and mailboxes. Assume that Mabel Garcia is a recreational skydiver, the payroll manager at Floss Recycling Incorporated, and likes to grow roses.

Mabel should use labels for these high-priority categories:

- Husband—messages from her husband
- Family—family correspondence
- Payroll—messages from colleagues in the payroll department
- Coworkers—messages from people at Floss Recycling, Inc. who are not in the payroll department
- Announce—company-wide announcements (that sometimes turn into to-do items)
- Friends—messages from friends
- Unknown—messages that her filters can't categorize

If Mabel uses Eudora for Mac OS, she will have enough labels for her medium-priority messages:

- ParachuteJumps—parachute jump announcement mailing list
- RoseGardening—rose gardening mailing list
- Parachuting—general skydiving mailing list
- ConfirmationsUpdates—merchandise order confirmations

Eudora for Mac OS even has enough labels for her low-priority messages:

- Humor—jokes
- ProbableJunkEmail—junk email

However, if Mabel uses Eudora for Windows, she won't have enough labels for her medium- and low-priority messages. She must group those messages in mailboxes.

You should move messages out of your inbox when you've finished with them, so you can see your "to-do" items more easily. If you transfer them to mailboxes with the same names as their labels, they will be easier to find. ("(Don't) Mark Messages Done by Deleting" on page 98 will talk more about saving old messages.) So even if you have enough labels for all of your categories, you still need to create some mailboxes.

(If you don't know how to create and delete mailboxes, please read "Mailboxes" on page 249, then come back to this page.)

Order Your Mailboxes

You might want to give mailboxes the exact same name as your labels. However, Eudora lists mailboxes in alphabetical order—which usually isn't the same as your priority order or the order of your labels. To make it easier to find a mailbox quickly, you might want to change the order of the mailboxes to match your priority order. To change your mailboxes' order, put a letter in front of the mailbox name:

Without Letter	**With Letter**
Announce	a-Husband
ConfirmationsUpdates	b-Family
Coworkers	h-Payroll
Family	i-Coworkers
Friends	j-Announce
Humor	m-Friends
Husband	p-ParachuteJumps
ParachuteJumps	q-Roses
Parachuting	r-Parachuting
Payroll	w-ConfirmationsUpdates
ProbableJunkEmail	y-Humor
RoseGardening	z-ProbableJunkEmail

Why aren't the letters consecutive? (For example, why doesn't Payroll start with c- instead of h-?) Because at some point, Mabel might want to add a new mailbox in between two old mailboxes. If she leaves a few letters unassigned, she can use an unassigned letter for the new mailbox instead of having to reassign all of the letters.

Eudora Filters

Once you have made labels and mailboxes for the different categories of your messages, you can start grouping your messages. Filters, like mail-sorting clerks, help enormously. (If you are already very familiar with filters in Eudora, you can skip to "Use Multiple Accounts to Group Messages" on page 57.)

When you become so rich and famous that you get a flood of paper mail, you will probably hire somebody to sort your mail. You'll ask him or her to put all your greeting cards in one box, all the bills in another box, all junk mail in the trash, and so on.

Filters can do similar sorting actions. Mail room clerks, however, are much smarter than computers, so you have to be much more precise with a filter. You could tell a mail clerk simply, "Put all junk mail in that box." With a filter, you'd have to say something like "When the envelope's finish is glossy, put that piece of mail into the box marked 'Junk'." In addition, a single filter can't handle too much at once. It's as if you needed one clerk to pick out junk mail and a second clerk to pick out bills.

"Real-World" Filters

To help introduce filters, let's first spend a page writing instructions for mail room clerks. For each instruction, you need to tell your clerks what action to take and under what conditions to take it. In the previous example, you want the clerk that when a letter arrives, if

```
the envelope's finish is glossy
```

then he or she should

```
put the piece of mail in the box labeled Junk
```

Or, combining the condition and the action:

```
when a letter arrives
if the envelope's finish is glossy
then put the piece of mail in the box labeled Junk
```

Email filters are very similar to these mail room clerks. You just have to tell them (carefully) what you want them to do.

How to Organize Messages with Eudora Filters

When you create filters for email, you can't use the same type of rules as you'd give a mail clerk. Email messages don't have envelopes or handwriting to give clues about the message's nature. However, filters can look for specific words or phrases in the message. This is a very powerful capability.

For example, if Mabel wants assign the label Payroll to all messages from Andy Jain (andy@flossrecycling.com), she can set up a filter to change the label if the From: header matches his email address:

> when a message arrives
> if From: is andy@flossrecycling.com
> then Make Label→Payroll

To create this filter, Mabel needs to first select the menu option Window→ Filters (Mac OS) or Tools→Filters (Windows). She will see a window like the one inFigure 2:

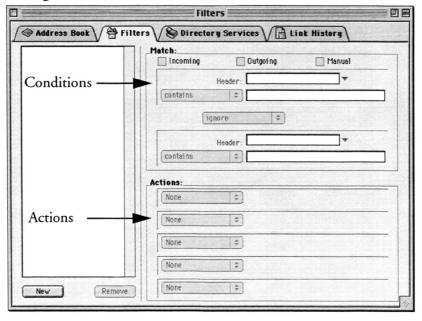

Figure 2: Blank Filters Window (Mac OS)

The Windows version is nearly identical except that the navigation tabs are at the bottom, as shown in Figure 3:

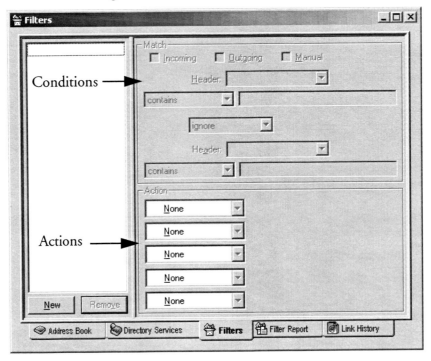

Figure 3: Blank Filters Window (Windows)

The Filters Window has several parts. On the left is a list of all the filters, with buttons at the bottom for creating new ones and deleting existing ones. Because Mabel doesn't have any filters yet, there aren't any filters in the lists in Figure 2 and Figure 3.

On the right-hand side is where Mabel sets up the filter conditions and actions. At the top of the right-hand side are three checkboxes labelled Incoming, Outgoing, and Manual. These boxes tell Eudora when to run the filters: on all incoming messages, on all outgoing messages, or on messages that Mabel selects.

If you put a check mark in the box labelled Manual at the top center of the Filters Window, then you can run that filter on messages at any time—not just when it arrives.

Outgoing filters are useful for keeping both sides of a conversation together. "How to Keep Conversations Together" on page 53 discusses outgoing filters further.

For now, Incoming is the only box Mabel needs. Fortunately, when she starts to create a new filter, Eudora puts a check mark in the Incoming box automatically.

Below the checkboxes are the filter's conditions, as indicated by the arrow marked Conditions in Figure 3 and Figure 4. Mabel can look for any word or phrase in any of several places in the message.

Below the conditions section is the actions section, indicated by the arrow marked Actions in Figure 3 and Figure 4.

To make the filter to assign the label Payroll to any message from Andy Jain (andy@flossrecycling.com) Mabel needs to first click on the New button. The name Untitled will appear in the list of filters in the left-hand side, as shown by the arrow in the upper left of Figure 4:

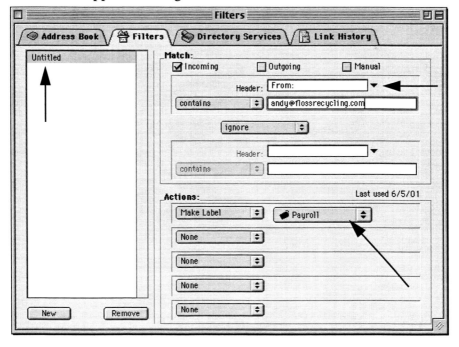

Figure 4: Assign Andy's Messages to Payroll Label

Changing the box next to Header: (shown by the arrow in the upper right of Figure 4) changes where the filter looks for the specified word or phrase. Mabel needs to change that box to From:. Directly below the header selection box is where Mabel enters the word or phrase that the filter looks for. In this case, Mabel should enter andy@flossrecycling.com.

Below the conditions section is the actions section. Filters can do up to five actions. The most important ones are Make Label (to assign a label to a message) and Transfer To (to move a message to another mailbox). "How to Prioritize with Advanced Filter Actions" on page 49 will cover other actions in more detail.

The only action Mabel's filter needs right now is an action that assigns the label Payroll to the message, as shown by the arrow in the lower right of Figure 4.

Finally, Mabel needs to save the filter by pressing Command-s (Mac OS) or Control-s (Windows). (She could also simply close the window; Eudora will ask if she wants to save her changes.)

How to Use Nicknames in Conditions to Reduce the Number of Filters

Suppose Mabel wants to assign the Payroll label to any messages from someone in the Payroll department, not just to Andy's messages. Mabel could make a different filter for each person in the Payroll department, but that would be a lot of work. Fortunately, Eudora filter conditions can find messages from a group of people by using nicknames.

If Mabel creates a nickname payroll in her Address book and puts all of the payroll department employees into that nickname, then she can automatically file all messages from her payroll department colleagues with a filter like this:

when a message arrives
if the sender is in the nickname payroll
then Make Label→Payroll

To make this filter, Mabel needs to change andy@flossrecycling.com to payroll and contains to intersects nickname, as shown by the arrow in Figure 5:

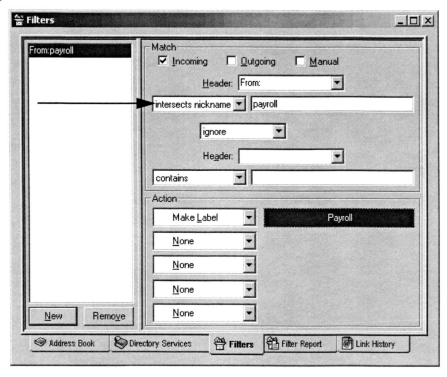

Figure 5: Find All Payroll Department Employees (Windows)

(Why "intersects nickname"? Because that's what Eudora's author decided to call it. Don't worry about the wording, just know that's how a filter checks to see if an address is in a nickname.)

How to Use Phrases to Find Coworkers

You can look for any words and phrases, not just email addresses. For example, suppose that messages from people inside Floss Recycling, Incorporated always have @flossrecycling.com in the return address. Mabel can then find all messages inside the company with this filter:

```
when a message arrives
if From: contains @flossrecycling.com
then Make Label→CoWorkers
```

This filter is very similar to the "Andy" filter in Figure 4, except for the text in the second box and the label, as shown by the two arrows in Figure 6:

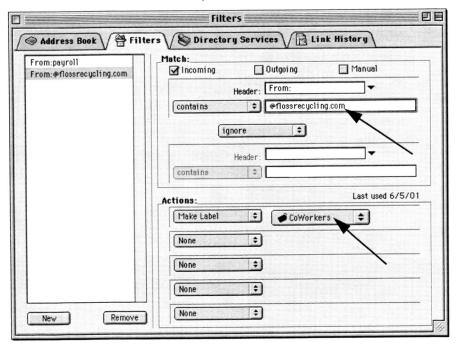

Figure 6: Condition to Find Internal Messages (MacOS)

Importance of Filter Order

Messages go through filters in the order that the filters are listed on the left of the Filters Window. So with the two filters that Mabel has now, all incoming messages first go through the Payroll filter and then through the CoWorkers filter. For example, suppose Andy sends a message to Mabel. The first filter assigns the label

Organize and Prioritize Your Messages

Payroll to Andy's message. But then the second message assigns the label CoWorkers to Andy's message—not what Mabel wants!

To stop messages from going through later filters, use the Skip Rest action, as shown by the lower arrow in Figure 7 and Figure 8:

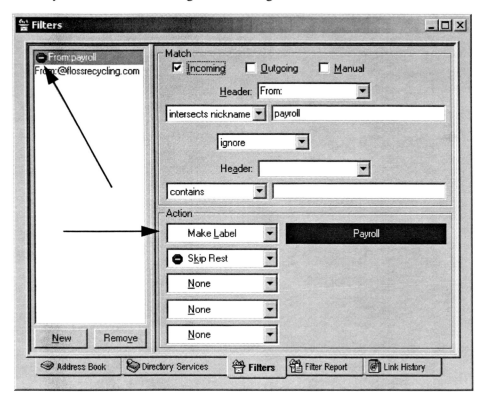

Figure 7: Skip Rest Action (Windows)

When a filter has a Skip Rest action, Eudora will put a mark in the list of filters. Eudora for Windows will display a small "stop sign" icon, as shown by the upper arrow in Figure 7. Eudora for Mac OS will display a little circle, as indicated by the upper arrow in Figure 8:

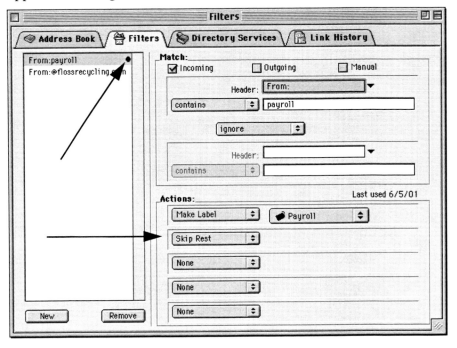

Figure 8: Skip Rest Action (Mac OS)

After a filter puts a message into a group—either by assigning a label or transferring the message to another mailbox—you should make sure that the filter stops.

How to Use «Any Recipient» to Find Mailing List Messages

There are many places besides the From: header where filters can look for a word or phrase. The most useful places to look for a word or phrase are Subject:, «Any Recipient», and «Body». For example, it is easy to find mailing list messages by looking for the mailing list address in «Any Recipient», as shown by the arrow in Figure 9:

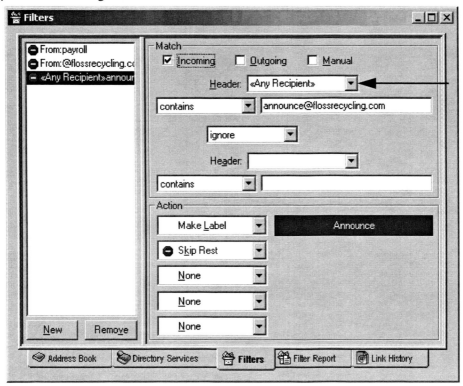

Figure 9: Find Mailing List Messages (Windows)

Your filters should almost always look for words and phrases in the «Any Recipient» header instead of the To: header. People sometimes put addresses in the Cc: header instead of the To: header, but «Any Recipient» will find words or phrases (or email addresses) in either.

Note that with the filter order shown in Figure 9, a message from Andy to the Announce mailing list will end up with the label Payroll. If the message is to the Announce mailing list, it probably isn't about payroll business. Mabel should drag the Announce filter to the top of the filter list so that the Payroll and CoWorkers filters don't keep Announce messages from getting filtered properly.

Make Filters More Precise By Combining Conditions

You've probably noticed that there is room for two conditions in the Filters Window. Combining conditions is not something that you will do frequently, but it is very handy sometimes.

For example, Mabel might not want to see messages that a car's lights are on unless it is *her* car. She could get rid of messages about other people's lights with a filter that transfers messages with the word headlights in the Subject: header to another mailbox—unless it has a description of her car in the Subject: header as well. To combine conditions for this filter, Mabel must change the bar that says ignore to say unless, as shown by the diagonal arrow in Figure 10. (You have the option of and, or, and unless.) Then Mabel must enter in the next condition:

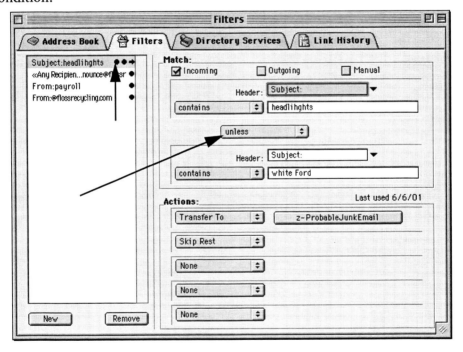

Figure 10: Filter for headlight messages (Mac OS)

Note that there are now two little circles and an arrow next to the headlights filter in the list of filters, as shown by the vertical arrow in Figure 10. With Eudora for Mac OS, filters that transfer a message to another mailbox do a Skip Rest

Organize and Prioritize Your Messages

automatically. Thus one of the little circles in Figure 10 is from the Transfer To action and one is from the Skip Rest. (The small arrow shows that the headlights filter has a Transfer To action.)

With Eudora for Windows, a Transfer To action will not stop later filters from acting on that message. To remind the Windows users how important Skip Rest is, I will show it even in Mac OS screen shots. (Even though Skip Rest isn't necessary in Mac OS filters that have a Transfer To action, it won't cause any problems if it is there.)

Separate "To-Do" Messages from "Done" Messages

People use email for more than just communicating. Almost everyone uses email to remind them of things they need to do. Many people even send themselves email to remind themselves to do something.

It is therefore critically important that you keep your "to-do" messages separate from the messages you are done with. For your high-priority messages (the ones in your inbox), the easiest way to mark them "done" is to move them to a different mailbox. Any messages that remain in the inbox are then either "to-do" items or Unread messages.

The easiest way to move messages out of the inbox is with manual filters. For example, Mabel could set up a manual filter to transfer messages from people in her payroll nickname into the h-Payroll mailbox. Then, when Mabel finishes with a Payroll message, she can transfer that message out of the inbox by manually filtering.

There are three ways to run all your manual filters on selected messages:

- press Command-j (Mac OS) or Control-j (Windows),
- select the menu command Special→Filter Messages, or
- put a button in the toolbar to filter messages and click on that button. (See "How to Put Buttons in the Toolbar" on page 95.)

To use this technique, Mabel needs a second filter for each of her high-priority categories. The filter that assigns the label must run only on incoming messages, while the filter that moves it to a mailbox must be manual only. For example, to file Payroll messages when she's done with them, Mabel needs a filter with a check mark in the Manual box, as shown in Figure 11:

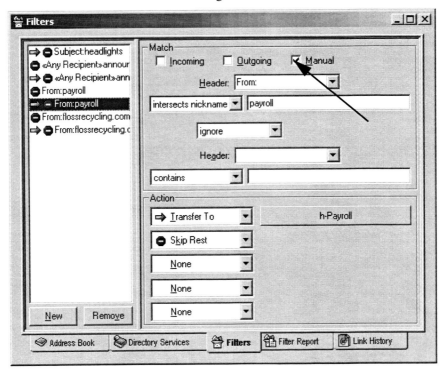

Figure 11: Manually Transfer Payroll Messages (Mac OS)

Medium-priority messages (which you transfer into mailboxes as soon as they arrive) by definition are not supposed to turn into "to-do" items very often. However, if you do have to respond to or act upon a message that isn't in the inbox, you can move it to the inbox to show that it is a "to-do" item. When you are done with it, transfer it back to its normal mailbox.

Because the incoming filter for that message transfers it to a mailbox, you don't need a separate manual filter. Instead, put a check mark in the Manual box of the existing filter.

I think that filtering manually when you are done with them is the simplest way to go through your messages. However, if you don't like this technique, you will learn more techniques in "Quickly Mark Messages 'Done' or 'To-Do'" on page 98.

Organize and Prioritize Your Messages

How to Prioritize with Advanced Filter Actions

By this point, you have learned the basics of organizing your messages with filters. You've seen how to use Make Label, Transfer to and Skip Rest to make categories' importance obvious. However, there are several additional filter actions that can help make messages' importance even more obvious:

- Open to open a message or its mailbox in its own window
- Make Priority to raise or lower the priority of a message
- Play Sound to let you hear what type of message arrives

TIP: One action that I do *not* think you should use is Transfer To→Trash. If you automatically delete messages, someday your filters will delete a message that you care about. It is much better to move suspected junk email to a mailbox, so you can occasionally look through the mailbox for misfiled messages.

This section's advice, while useful, isn't as critical as the sections you've already read. If you are in a hurry, you can skip to "How to Keep Conversations Together" on page 53 for now.

How to Show Importance by (Not) Opening Messages and Mailboxes

Eudora normally opens all mailboxes that have new messages. If you don't want to be bothered by low-priority messages, you might want to turn that feature off and use filters to open your medium-priority mailboxes. (You will probably leave your inbox open all the time, so you should not need to open it with filters.)

Select Special→ Settings…→Get Attention (Mac OS) or Tools→Options…→Get Attention (Windows). Uncheck the box next to Open mailbox. Then, to make your filters open your medium-priority mailboxes, select the filter action `Open` and put a checkmark in the box next to `Mailbox`, as shown by the arrow in Figure 12:

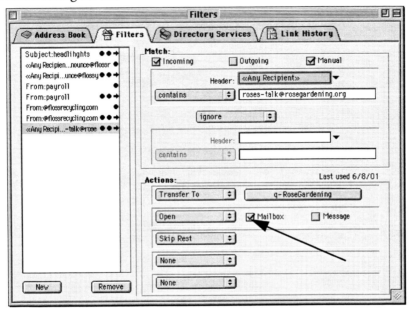

Figure 12: Filter to Open Mailbox (MacOS)

If a message is *really* important, you might want to open it in its own window. Select the filter action `Open` and put a checkmark in the box next to `Message`. Mabel might want her filters to open messages from her husband in their own window, not open `z-ProbableJunkEmail` or `y-Humor` at all, and open the mailbox for all other incoming messages.

How to Make Importance More Obvious with the "Make Priority" Action

Eudora can attach a priority level to a message. These priorities usually reflect the priority that the sender thinks a message should have. The priority is shown as arrows up or down in a mailbox' second column (just to the right of the blue `Unread` balls).

Your filters can override the priority level of messages with the `Make Priority` action. The advantage of overriding the priority level is that the new priority level is more likely to reflect your opinion of the message's true priority. The disadvantage is that you can't tell what the sender thought the priority level was. Frequently, however, the sender's opinion of the priority level is very different from your opinion, so you might not mind.

If you aren't comfortable throwing away the sender's priority, you can set the priority relative to the old priority. You can Raise or Lower the priority. This takes into account both your priority and the sender's priority.

For example, Mabel might want to use Make Priority to lower the priority of anything marked FYI (For Your Information), as shown in Figure 13:

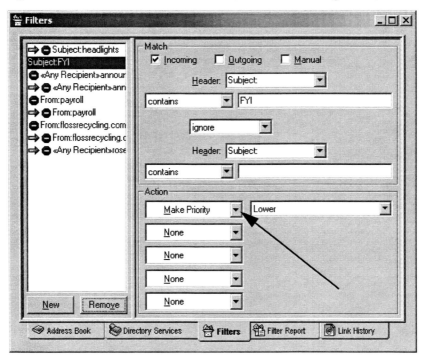

Figure 13: Lowering the Priority for FYI Messages (Windows)

How to Hear Importance with the "Play Sound" Action

If your filters play sounds, you can tell when important messages come in, even if you're not focusing on your computer. For example, if a message from Mabel's rose gardening mailing list arrives, she probably won't put aside what she's doing to read it. If a message from someone in the Payroll department announces itself, she probably will.

If a sound has some connection to its category, it's easier to remember what the sound means. For example, you might associate the following sounds and message types:

- old-fashioned cash register ring or credit card slider sound for sale confirmations
- laughter for jokes
- rude noises for junk mail
- wedding bells for messages from your spouse.

To play a sound, set an action to Play Sound, as shown by the arrow in Figure 14

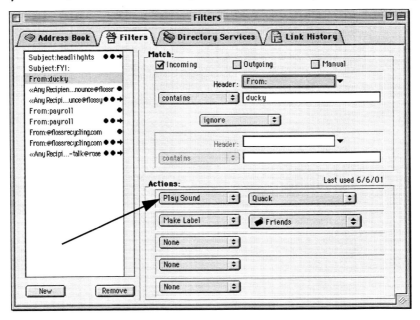

Figure 14: Play Sound example (Mac OS)

TIP: If your coworkers can hear every sound that your computer makes, they might get annoyed if you attach sounds to your messages. Use headphones or don't play sounds.

If you have your filters play sounds, make sure that the sounds are very short—shorter than the time it takes to say the phrase "filter action." Your sounds will play over and over, and you will get tired of waiting for long sounds to finish.

By default, Eudora plays a sound when a new message arrives. You can disable this by changing the Get Attention page in the settings. Select Special→Settings...→Get Attention (Mac OS) or Tools→Options...→Get Attention (Windows) and uncheck the box next to Play a sound.

TIP: You should disable your filter sounds before you check a big backlog of messages. Otherwise, you might have to wait for a very long time for the sounds to finish.

How to Keep Conversations Together

The filters you've learned so far are good for organizing messages that you receive. It is also helpful to put outgoing messages in the same mailbox as related incoming messages. There are two ways to do this: by making outgoing filters for all of your high- and medium-priority categories and by using Eudora's Fcc (Folder Carbon Copy) option.

Moving messages out of your Out box also might improve Eudora's performance. Eudora keeps all of the messages in your In, Out, and Trash mailboxes in memory. If any of those mailboxes get large, the memory demands can reduce Eudora's performance.

How to Keep Conversations Together with Filters

You can set up any filter to operate on outgoing messages by checking the Outgoing checkbox in the Filters Window. For example, Mabel could make a filter that moves all outgoing messages to anyone in the Payroll department into the h-Payroll mailbox with a filter like the one in Figure 15:

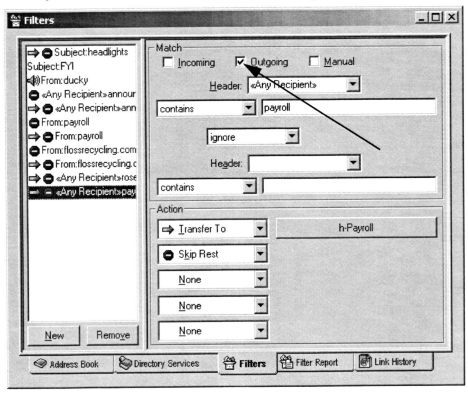

Figure 15: Outgoing Payroll Message Filter (Mac OS)

How to Keep Incoming and Outgoing Messages Together with FCC

With the Fcc (File Carbon Copy) option, Eudora files any reply of yours in the same mailbox as the message you replied to—except if the original message is in the inbox. To use the Fcc option, select Special→ Settings…→Sending Mail (Mac OS) or Tools→Options…→Replying (Windows) and put a check mark in the box labelled Automatically Fcc to original mailbox, as shown by the arrows in Figures 16 and 17:

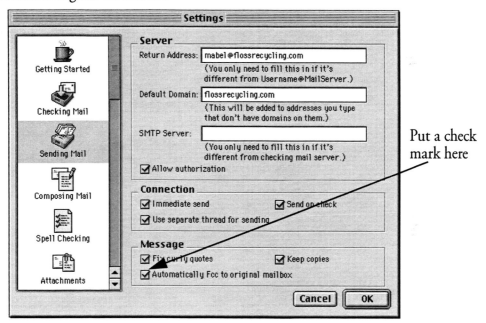

Figure 16: Automatically Fcc to Original mailbox (Mac OS)

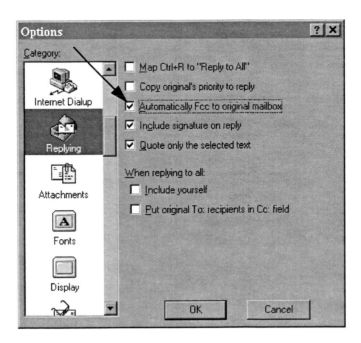

Figure 17: Automatically Fcc to Original Mailbox (Windows)

Telling Eudora to automatically Fcc messages to will only do part of the job: messages that are not replies will still end up in your Out mailbox. Still, it is much easier to put one check mark into one box than to create a lot of outgoing mail filters.

How to Test Your Filters

It is a good idea to test your filters when you set them up. If you make a mistake, your filters could put an important message into a mailbox that you never look at.

Manual filters are extremely useful for testing your filters. You should probably put a check in the Manual checkbox in all the filters *except* for your high-priority filters—the ones that change the label and leave the message in the inbox. (If you put a check in the Manual checkbox for messages that stay in the inbox, you won't be able to use manual filtering to move those messages out of the inbox as described in "Separate 'To-Do' Messages from 'Done' Messages on page 47.)

Organize and Prioritize Your Messages

If you need to test your high-priority filters, you can put a check mark temporarily in the Manual checkbox. Be sure to uncheck the Manual box when you are done testing.

If you are using Eudora for Mac OS and your filters don't do what you expect, you can find out which filters a message activates. Select a message, hold down the Shift key, and then open the Filters window. Eudora will highlight all the filters whose conditions match the selected message.

If a filter's condition appears to be correct, but the filter didn't do the appropriate action when you ran it manually, make sure that the Manual box is checked. It is very easy to forget to check the Manual box—even I do so with astonishing regularity.

Use Multiple Accounts to Group Messages

If setting up filters looks like too much work for you to do right now, you can use multiple email accounts to group your messages. You can frequently check the accounts that you use for higher-priority topics and only occasionally check your low-priority accounts.

In the past, having multiple email accounts was very expensive, but there are now numerous free Web-based email services. Furthermore, some of the Web-based services block junk email.

However, there are significant disadvantages to using free Web-based accounts:

- You have to check each account.
- Free services usually make you look at advertising.
- A free service might limit how many messages you can keep or how much disk space you can use.

Eudora will let you check messages from multiple accounts by using different *personalities*. (Select Help→Using Personalities (Mac OS) or Help→Topics→Index→personalities (Windows) to learn more about personalities.) Using Eudora to check the messages in all your accounts might make it easier to check your messages, but you would need to routinely switch between your different personalities. The more personalities you have, the harder it is to remember which personality you are using at any given moment.

You should have very few accounts—probably less than five. I recommend using three accounts: your work account, a personal account, and an account for junk mail.

Personal Accounts

Separating your work and personal email is one of the best things you can do. Besides making it easier to concentrate on work issues while you are at work, it has these benefits:

- If you suddenly lose your job, you won't also lose all the addresses in your email address book.
- Your personal email is more private. In some places, employers have the legal right to read email on your work computer at any time without your permission or knowledge. If your employer gets sued, lawyers from both sides might end up reading all your company email—regardless of whether it is related to the suit or even your work.
- You are less likely to get in trouble for using company time and equipment for personal use.

If you get a personal account, always checking it from your work copy of Eudora (by using different personalities) eliminates many of these benefits. It's better to use a web-based email system for your personal email or to only download personal messages to your home computer.

Junk Mail Accounts

Junk mailers have programs that scan the Web for email addresses. If your email address gets onto a Web page in any way—if you put it on a home page or if you post a message to a discussion group that is archived on the Web—junk mailers will find you.

Similarly, if you give a retailer your email address, they might send you advertisements in the future. They might also sell your address to other retailers. Even if they have a privacy policy that says that they won't give your address to anyone else, the privacy policy isn't guaranteed to continue if the company goes

Organize and Prioritize Your Messages

bankrupt. When a company files for bankruptcy, knowledge of your email address is considered part of the company's assets and might be sold to pay off creditors.

Therefore, you should have at least one account to give to Web sites and other retailers.

Summary

- Prioritizing and organizing messages can help you read email more efficiently. Filters can automatically categorize your messages before you read them.
- People usually have a hard time keeping track of "to-do" messages if they use filters to transfer all their messages out of their inbox. For messages that might turn into "to-do" items, you should assign them a label, leave them in your inbox, and sort your inbox by label.
- Good paper filing strategies are different from good email filing strategies. You should have far fewer categories for your email messages than you would for the same number of paper memos.
- Sorting messages by the sender's group is an effective strategy.
- Changing the name of a mailbox changes where it appears in the list of mailboxes.
- Nicknames are useful for filtering messages.
- The order of your filters affects the filtering behavior.
- You can use manual filters to transfer messages you've finished with out of the inbox.
- Test your filters by manually filtering messages.
- Fcc (Folder Carbon Copy) can put many of your responses with their related messages. Outgoing filters take more work, but do an even better job of keeping conversations together.
- You can file messages simply and cheaply by using multiple accounts. Using multiple accounts isn't as complicated as setting up filters, but isn't as powerful.

CHAPTER 3

Useful Filter Recipes

Filters are most effective when messages are very regular and predictable. Fortunately, most types of message have some consistency to them. This chapter shows examples of the regularity in several types of message and how to use that predictability to create useful filters.

This chapter is designed to be a "cookbook" for you to follow when setting up your own filters. Thus, you should save this chapter for a time when you are sitting at your computer. Skipping this chapter right now won't hurt your understanding of later chapters.

Filter Order

As mentioned briefly earlier, the order of filters is very important. Filters should handle messages in an order something like this:

- call attention to executable attachments
- adjust priority (without moving to a mailbox)
- file jokes
- file mailing list messages
- file confirmation messages
- file messages from people you correspond with regularly
- file messages from other people you know
- file junk email
- keep related incoming and outgoing messages together

Putting the filters for mailing lists near the beginning of the list of filters will help organize messages properly for people who have two or more different roles. For example, suppose Mabel's sister is on the roses-talk mailing list. Mabel probably wants to keep her sister's messages about roses with the other roses messages, not mixed in with messages about who is going to pick Mother up from the train station. Thus Mabel needs to put her "roses" filter before her "family" filter.

Be sure to put your unsolicited commercial email filters near the *end* of your filter list so that you don't accidentally misfile important messages. For example, both junk email and mailing list messages frequently contain instructions on how to unsubscribe. If your mailing list filters are before your junk email filters, you can check for unsubscribe in a junk email filter without the risk of treating your mailing list messages like junk email.

The filter recipes in this chapter appear in the same order that they should appear in Eudora's filter list.

Example Recipes

Because it is much easier to modify a filter than to create one from the beginning, I put a file with this chapters' filter recipes at:

    http://www.OvercomeEmailOverload.com/eudora/filters.html

You can download those filters and modify the rules for your own needs. **Be sure to read the directions on the Web page!**

Notation

Figures showing Eudora windows have inherently lower resolution than regular text and take up a lot of space. For that reason, I show all of the filter recipes in regular text, similar to the recipes on page 36. There are some screen shots to reinforce the textual recipes.

Each filter recipe is double-boxed and looks something like this:

> when *time*
> if *condition*
> then *actions*

For actions that have two parts, the two menu selections are joined by an arrow (→).

For example:

> when the message comes in or manual filtering is selected
> if `From:` is `mabel@flossrecycling.com`
> then `Transfer To`→`NotesToMeFromMe`

TIP: Don't forget to test your filters, as discussed in "How to Test Your Filters" on page 56.

Notes

Because noises are personal preferences and depend upon what sound files you have on your system, I don't show them in filter recipes. Add sounds as you like.

Also, because the Windows version of Eudora only has seven labels, I only use seven labels in the examples.

As in Chapter 2, this chapter uses the fictional Mabel Garcia in the examples.

The rest of this chapter shows filter recipes.

Find .EXE Files

Executable files are very dangerous. While virus writers rarely write viruses for the Macintosh any more, the number of Windows viruses keeps growing.

Eudora is more secure than many email programs. It doesn't allow Visual Basic scripting, and opening or previewing a message doesn't automatically open its attachments. However, if you are running Windows and click on a virus-infested .EXE file, you can get infected. Ideally, you'd like to quarantine .EXE files and get a warning about them.

Oddly, it is easier to quarantine .EXE files with Eudora for Mac OS than with Eudora for Windows. With Eudora for Windows, it's harder to spot .EXEs and you can't do as much with them when you find them.

How to Quarantine .EXE Files with Eudora for Mac OS

For every attachment, Eudora adds a line of text to the body of its message. Under Mac OS, the line looks something like this:

```
Attachment converted: "hh.exe" (bina/mdos)
```

Under Mac OS, Eudora can move all of a message's attachments from the Attachments Finder folder to a different Finder folder. (Note: "folder" here does not refer to a collection of mailboxes, but one of the folders that Mac OS manages.)

While it might be tempting to transfer all of a message's attachments to the Trash if any of them are .EXE files, you shouldn't. A message might have one executable attachment and six attachments you want. A better strategy is to quarantine all the attachments for that message in a separate disk folder.

Thus a filter for quarantining .EXEs would look something like this:

```
when the message comes in or manual filtering is selected
if «Body» contains .exe" (bina/mdos)
then Move Attachments To→Attachments:EXEs and Skip Rest
```

Note that while there are quotation marks after .exe, there are *not* supposed to be quotation marks before .exe.

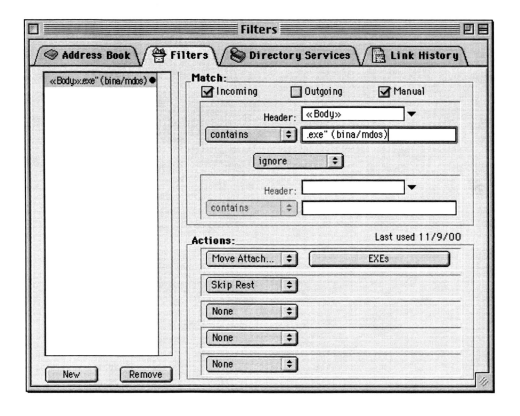

Figure 18: Quarantining .EXE Files (Mac OS)

How to Quarantine .EXE with Eudora for Windows

When Eudora for Windows decodes an attachment, it adds a line of text that looks something like this:

```
Attachment Converted: "C:\PROGRAMS\EUDORA\ATTACHMENTS\HH.EXE"
```

Unfortunately, there isn't much under Windows that you can do with an .EXE file once you've found it. The best you can do is put the message in a quarantine mailbox:

when the message comes in or manual filtering is selected
if «Body» contains `Attachment Converted` and
    «Body» contains `.exe"`
then `Play Sound`→(something obnoxious),
    `Transfer To`→`z-Quarantine`, `Open Mailbox`, and `Skip Rest`

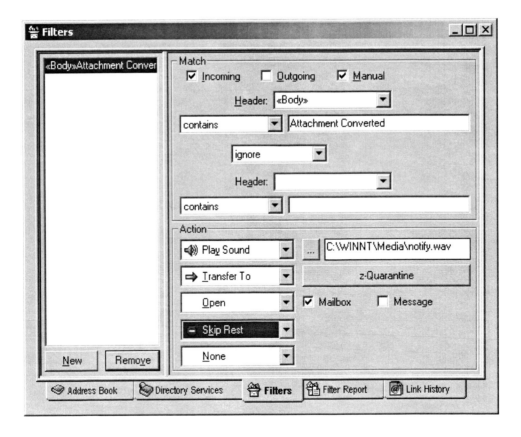

Figure 19: Making .EXE Files Obvious (Windows)

     Useful Filter Recipes

Adjust the Priority Level

One easy way to adjust a message's priority is to look for common keywords that people use in `Subject:` headers.

You might want to lower the priority level of any messages with `FYI:` (For Your Information) or `BTW:` (By The Way) in the subject. These usually contain information that you don't need to respond to, like

```
Subject: FYI: donuts in break room

The donut fairy left a dozen glazed donuts in the break
room by conference room C2. Enjoy!
```

or

```
Subject: BTW: donuts are stale

Don't bother getting up -- the donuts by C2 are extremely
stale.
```

Therefore, you might enjoy this filter:

```
when the message comes in or manual filtering is selected
if Subject: contains BTW: or Subject: contains FYI:,
then Make Priority→Lower
```

You might want to raise the priority level for messages that request actions. These frequently have subject headers starting with `REQ:` or `ACTION REQUIRED:`

```
Subject: REQ: new donut fairy

Please post a help wanted ad for a new donut fairy.
```

You might want a filter like this:

> when the message comes in or manual filtering is selected
> if `Subject:` contains `REQ:` or `Subject:` contains `ACTION REQUIRED:`
> then `Make Priority`→`Raise`

Alert readers may notice that the action in this section's filters do not have "and `Skip Rest`" at the end. The guideline I suggest is to stop *after the Eudora filters the message into a group or category.* Here, Mabel might want to use a later filter to move the message into a mailbox.

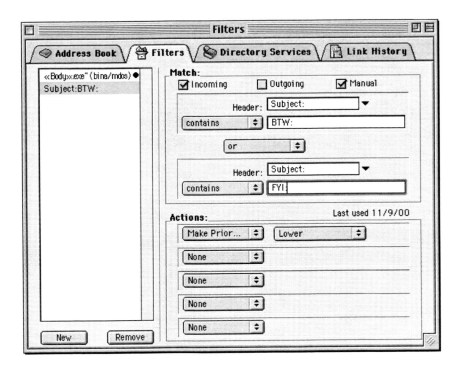

Figure 20: Filter for FYI and BTW (Mac OS)

Lower the Priority Level of Multiply Forwarded Messages

Occasionally, unsuspecting people will forward hoaxes, chain letters, or jokes to everyone that they know. (Chapter 5, *Reduce the Number of Incoming Messages*, discusses such nuisance messages in more detail.) Messages with many forwards are probably not a high priority:

```
Subject: Fwd: FW: FW: Fwd: dihydrogen oxide!!!!!

>>>A friend of mine at the university told me that they've
>>>discovered dihydrogen oxide in every brand of coffee!
>>>Send this to everyone you know and then stop drinking
>>>coffee!!!!
```

To help recognize such nuisance messages, look for all combinations of Fw: and Fwd: and for multiple greater-than signs:

when the message comes in or manual filtering is selected if Subject: contains FW:FW: or Subject: contains Fwd: Fwd: then Make Priority→Lower
when the message comes in or manual filtering is selected if Subject: contains Fwd:FW: or Subject: contains FW: Fwd: then Make Priority→Lower
when the message comes in or manual filtering is selected if «Body» contains >>> then Make Priority→Lower

Instead of lowering the priority level, you could put multiply-forwarded messages into their own mailbox. (If you move them into their own mailbox, remember to add a Skip Rest action at the end of the condition.)

File Jokes

Because jokes are so easy to redistribute by email, people do. If you're lucky, people will put HUMOR: at the beginning of the subject header. You can put those jokes into a special mailbox to read later:

> when the message comes in or manual filtering is selected
> if Subject: contains HUMOR:,
> then Transfer To→y-Humor and Skip Rest

Sometimes you'll have one friend who forwards a lot of jokes to all his or her friends. You might be able to save the friendship with a filter like this:

> when the message comes in or manual filtering is selected
> if From: is loretta@facelessentity.com and
>   Subject: starts with FWD:,
> then Transfer To→y-Humor and Skip Rest

If the friend always sends the jokes to the same list of people, you could also try looking for someone in the To: header that you never correspond with:

> when the message comes in or manual filtering is selected
> if From: is loretta@facelessentity.com and
>   To: contains froglet32@ueci-h.edu,
> then Transfer To→y-Humor and Skip Rest

File Mailing Lists

Because mailing lists can generate an enormous number of messages, filtering mailing lists can be very helpful. Fortunately, mailing list messages are usually very regular and so easy to filter.

Mailing lists almost always have the same addressee, so check for that address in «Any Recipient». For example, these filters will categorize or file all of the messages on Mabel's company announcements and rose gardening mailing lists:

when the message comes in if «Any Recipient» contains announce@flossrecycling.com then Make Label→Announce, Open→Mailbox, and Skip Rest
when manual filtering is selected if «Any Recipient» contains announce@flossrecycling.com then Transfer To→j-Announce, Open→Mailbox, and Skip Rest
when the message comes in or manual filtering is selected if «Any Recipient» contains roses-talk@rosegardens.org then Transfer To→q-RoseGardening, Open→Mailbox, and Skip Rest

Note that because Mabel has a label for the announcements list, there are two announcements filters. When the message arrives, the first filter gives it the Announce label. When Mabel is done with the message, she can press Command/Control-j to send the message through the second filter, moving the message to the mailbox j-Announce.

File Confirmations and Updates

If you buy things online, you may get computer-generated notifications that orders have shipped, notices of upcoming sales, and so on. If you are on mailing lists, you may get email from time to time from the list administrator. You might want to make a nickname that has all the email addresses for such special messages. You can then use that nickname to put such messages in their own mailbox:

> when the message comes in or manual filtering is selected
>
> if From: intersects nickname ConfirmationsAndUpdates,
>
> then Transfer To→w-ConfirmationsUpdates, Open→Mailbox, and
>
>   Skip Rest

(For more on mailing list confirmations, see "Mailing List Administration" on page 111.

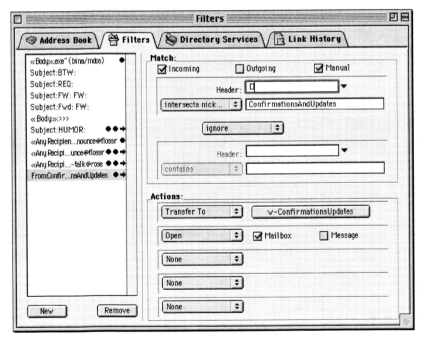

Figure 21: Confirmations And Updates Filter (Mac OS)

                          Useful Filter Recipes

File Frequent Correspondents

There may be people that you correspond with so frequently that you have labels for them, as discussed in "Group by Category" on page 30. Each category has two filters, as discussed in "Separate 'To-Do' Messages from 'Done' Messages" on page 47. Mabel can filter messages from important people in her life with filters like these:

when the message comes in if From: contains `charlie@electricbagpipes.com`, then `Make Label`→`Charlie` and `Skip Rest`
when manual filtering is selected if From: contains `charlie@electricbagpipes.com`, then `Transfer To`→`a-Charlie` and `Skip Rest`
when the message comes in if From: intersects nickname `family`, then `Make Label`→`Family` and `Skip Rest`
when manual filtering is selected if From: intersects nickname `family`, then `Transfer To`→`b-Family` and `Skip Rest`
when the message comes in if From: intersects nickname `payroll`, then `Make Label`→`Payroll` and `Skip Rest`
when manual filtering is selected if From: intersects nickname `payroll`, then `Transfer To`→`h-Payroll` and `Skip Rest`
when the message comes in if From: intersects nickname `friends`, then `Make Label`→`Friends` and `Skip Rest`
when manual filtering is selected if From: intersects nickname `friends`, then `Transfer To`→`m-Friends` and `Skip Rest`

File Messages from Coworkers

Filters can almost always recognize people inside your company or organization easily. Look at the From: header of an internal message and see what the format of internal addresses is.

Internal messages might have your company's name in the return address, like pat@flossrecycling.com or pat@toothpaste.flossrecycling.com. If so, use two filters like this:

when the message comes in if From: contains flossrecycling.com, then Make Label→CoWorkers and Skip Rest
when manual filtering is selected if From: contains flossrecycling.com, then Transfer To→i-CoWorkers and Skip Rest

Internal addresses might not have an @ at all. (The @ usually isn't needed when the sender and receiver have their mail accounts on the same computer.) For example, an internal email address might appear simply as pat. In that case, use two filters like this:

when the message comes in if From: does not contain @, then Make Label→CoWorkers and Skip Rest
when manual filtering is selected if From: does not contain @, then Transfer To→i-CoWorkers and Skip Rest

Finally, there might be an @ but not the company domain, like pat@toothpaste. This is harder to catch with a filter. You may be able to use a filter that looks for anything that doesn't contain "dot-something"—.com, .net, .org, .uk, and so on:

when the message comes in if From: doesn't contain., then Make Label→CoWorkers, and Skip Rest
when manual filtering is selected if From: doesn't contain., then Transfer To→i-CoWorkers, and Skip Rest

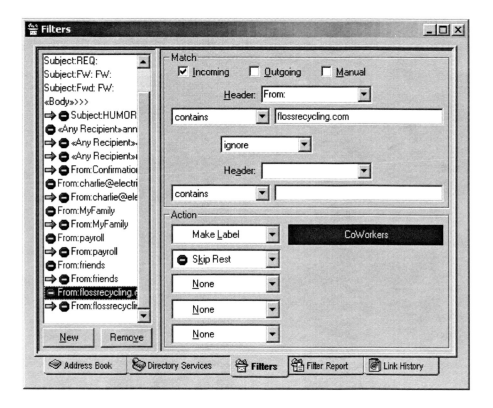

Figure 22: Filter for Messages Inside the Company (Windows)

Skip Messages from People You Know

It is a good idea to put in a filter that stops when it finds someone you know. That will help keep messages from your friends from accidentally getting filtered as "nuisance" email.

> when the message comes in or manual filtering is selected
> if From: intersects nickname EveryoneIKnow,
> then Skip Rest

All messages that continue past this filter are then likely to be junk email.

This does mean that you have to maintain a group nickname of everyone you know, but that can be much more pleasant than getting lots of junk email.

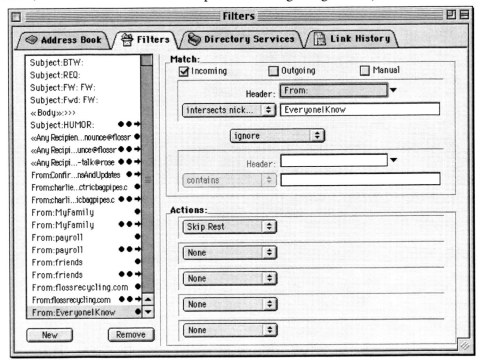

Figure 23: Filter for People You Know (Mac OS)

File Junk

Junk email can be a big contributor to email overload. Junk email—also called *spam* or *UCE* (Unsolicited Commercial Email)—wastes not just your time but also your emotional energy.

Getting lots of messages like this is tiring:

```
Subject: ADV: Make Money In Your Spare Time!!

MAKE MONEY FAST by selling Ostrich Meat from Your Own
Home!!!

Ostrich meat is LO-FAT, tasty, and NUTRICIOUS! Everybody is
going to want to try Ostrich Meat and SOON! Your never
going to get a better chance of getting RICH while working
in YOUR OWN HOME!! For more info on how you can become
WEALTHY, at mail to:
OstrichMeat@OpportunityKnocks.Boise.ID.US!

This message is sent in compliance of the new e-mail bill
Section 301. Per Section 301, Paragraph (a)(2)(C) of S.
1618. If you have received this message in error, or do not
wish to receive further messages, please reply and type
"Remove" in the subject line. Your request to be removed
will be processed within 24 hours.
```

Fortunately, there are several common patterns in junk email that filters can recognize. Unsolicited commercial email messages frequently have:

- the word ADV (as in ADVertisement) in the subject header
- language that insists that you can make large sums of money quickly
- strong language insisting that this is not a multi-level marketing scheme (but which it usually is)
- mention of credit cards
- instructions (usually incorrect) on how to stop getting email from this source in the future
- the statement that the message complies with junk email regulations

Unsolicited commercial email seems to have a very high density of capital letters, exclamation points (!) and poor grammar, but it is difficult to write filters in Eudora (or any consumer-grade email program) to recognize those features.

TIP: **In most cases, you should not set up filters to delete junk email.** Instead, move junk email to a mailbox. That protects you from mistakes in your filters. Once a week or so, look over the subject headers in the junk email mailbox to look for misfiled messages. After you deal with any incorrectly filed messages, you can delete the whole batch of accumulated junk email at once.

Here are some filters that find junk email and move it to a low-priority mailbox:

when the message comes in or manual filtering is selected if «Body» contains `make money fast` or   «Body» contains `multi-level marketing` then `Transfer To→z-ProbableJunkEmail` and `Skip Rest`
when the message comes in or manual filtering is selected if «Body» contains `unsubscribe in the subject` or   «Body» contains `the word remove in the subject` then `Transfer To→z-ProbableJunkEmail` and `Skip Rest`
when the message comes in or manual filtering is selected if «Body» contains `to be removed from this list` or   «Body» contains `section 301, Paragraph` then `Transfer To→z-ProbableJunkEmail` and `Skip Rest`
when the message comes in or manual filtering is selected if «Body» contains "remove" `in the subject` or `Subject: contains ADV` then `Transfer To→z-ProbableJunkEmail` and `Skip Rest`
when the message comes in or manual filtering is selected if «Body» contains `you do not wish to receive further` then `Transfer To→z-ProbableJunkEmail` and `Skip Rest`

when the message comes in or manual filtering is selected if «Body» contains 1-900 or «Body» contains all major credit cards then Transfer To→z-ProbableJunkEmail and Skip Rest
when the message comes in or manual filtering is selected if «Body» contains Visa and «Body» contains Mastercard then Transfer To→z-ProbableJunkEmail and Skip Rest

TIP: "Unsubscribe" can show up in many legitimate messages. Do not use the word "unsubscribe" in your junk filters unless you have earlier filters that do a good job of finding legitimate messages, like the ones on page 71, page 73, page 74, and page 76.

Many junk messages advertise pornographic services and sites. For example:

```
Subject: Hi Sexy, I am lonely waiting for you to call me.

Hi Sexy Im lonely waiting for you to call me. Let me ad "a
little spice" to your life!
WARNING!!
These lines are extremely xxx-rated. Adults over 18 only!!!
Sex starved girls will give you a hot sexual experience
you'll never forget. Not recommended for people with weak
hearts or bad backs!!!
------------------------------------------------------------
-
Call 1-800-555-6666                    $2.99-$4.99 per min.
Visa/Mastercard/Amex                   Must be over 18
```

Advertisements for pornography frequently have:

- a notice that the message is only for people over a certain age (usually 18)
- the words sex, xxx, hot, babe, hardcore, and girls

Some useful filters for pornographic junk email are:

when the message comes in or manual filtering is selected if `Subject:` contains XXX or `Subject:` contains sex then `Transfer To`→`z-ProbableJunkEmail` and `Skip Rest`
when the message comes in or manual filtering is selected if «Body» contains must be over 18 or «Body» contains must be over 21 then `Transfer To`→`z-ProbableJunkEmail` and `Skip Rest`
when the message comes in or manual filtering is selected if «Body» contains adults only or «Body» contains sexiest then `Transfer To`→`z-ProbableJunkEmail` and `Skip Rest`
when the message comes in or manual filtering is selected if «Body» contains hardcore or «Body» contains hard core then `Transfer To`→`z-ProbableJunkEmail` and `Skip Rest`
when the message comes in or manual filtering is selected if «Body» contains girls and «Body» contains sex then `Transfer To`→`z-ProbableJunkEmail` and `Skip Rest`
when the message comes in or manual filtering is selected if «Body» contains hot and «Body» contains sex then `Transfer To`→`z-ProbableJunkEmail` and `Skip Rest`

Here is an example of why you shouldn't automatically delete junk email:

Subject: family news

It's been unusually **hot** here this week. The **girls** and Frank
are just lying around in the basement trying to stay cool.

Did you hear the news? My niece Diana is expecting in July!
I don't know what the baby's **sex** is yet. Boy, it seems like
only yesterday that I was taking Diana to the beach, but
she **must be over 18 by now**. (**Adults only** *think* that
their nieces stay children forever!)

By the way, I baked another batch of pumpkin bread -- my
garden is producing a huge number of pumpkins! I would
understand if you **do not wish to receive further** loaves,
so let me know if you don't want me to send you more.

The body of this message contains hot, girls, sex, must be over 18, adults
only and do not wish to receive further, but if you let filters delete this
message automatically, you'll keep getting pumpkin bread!

Blacklist Junk Emailers

If someone sent you junk email once, you probably don't want to read anything from that address ever again. One way you can filter junk email is by keeping a list of addresses that have sent you junk email before. If you add junk emailers to the nickname KnownSpammer, you can catch all future messages from those addresses with this filter:

> when the message comes in or manual filtering is selected
> if From: intersects nickname KnownSpammers,
> then Transfer To→z-ProbableJunkEmail and Skip Rest

Even if you have to maintain the KnownSpammer nickname by hand, this type of filter can be very satisfying.

While I know I just said that you shouldn't use filters to delete messages, I will grant a limited exception in this case. Once you have made absolutely certain that your filter for known spammers is working properly, you might want to change the action to delete the messages. Eudora gives a warning if you try to delete unread messages, so you may also want to mark the message Read first:

> when the message comes in or manual filtering is selected
> if From: intersects nickname KnownSpammer,
> then Make Status→Read, Transfer To→Trash, and Skip Rest

TIP: Sadly, it probably isn't worth your time to put free accounts (like hotbabes92347@yahoo.com) into your KnownSpammer nickname by hand because they'll probably send their next message from a different free account.

Aggressive Junk Email Filters (Windows Only)

Eudora 5 for Windows can look for messages that match a regular expression—a *pattern* of characters. Regular expressions are very powerful, but they are tricky to create. Furthermore, the regular expressions don't work quite as advertised as of Eudora 5.1. You should not experiment with regular expressions in Eudora unless you are a regular expressions expert already.

I've tested the filters in this section, and they catch a lot of junk email. However, these filters are aggressive enough that you need to be careful: they can easily catch legitimate messages as well. Use these filters *only* if earlier filters catch all of the people you know and care about *and* if you regularly look in your `z-ProbableJunkEmail` mailbox for mistakes.

For some reason, a lot of junk email messages have subjects that end in a number, like:

```
Subject: Make a FORTUNE selling OSTRICH MEAT!!!        7352
```

A filter that looks for a digit at the end of the subject will catch this message, but will also catch messages with subjects like:

```
Subject: Rose Gardening Meeting 8 PM, Tuesday, May 3
```

Looking for three digits is safer, but will still catch messages that end in a year, such as:

```
Subject: Rose Gardening Meeting 8 PM, Tuesday, May 3, 2038
```

Because now most years will start with a "2", your filter should look for three digits at the end of the subject that do not have a "2" in front of them. The filter for this is:

```
when the message comes in or manual filtering is selected
if Subject: matches regexp [013-9 ][0-9][0-9][0-9]$
then Transfer To→z-ProbableJunkEmail and Skip Rest
```

Note that there is a space after the first 9 in the filter condition. (See Help→Topics→Find→regexp for an explanation on what all those symbols mean—or just trust me that the filter works.)

Another unusual feature of junk email is that frequently the From: line doesn't have a "real name" in it. Legitimate correspondents usually have From: lines that look like this:

    From: "Mabel Garcia" <mabel@flossrecycling.com>

(sometimes without the quotation marks). Junk email, however, often has From: headers like this:

    From: aslk2387sj9@facelessentity.com

or this:

    From: <aslk2387sj9@facelessentity.com>

There are currently two types of common, legitimate messages that don't have "real names": messages from AOL users and messages from Web-based mailing lists. It is important that you have an earlier filter to catch mailing list messages and to check for AOL users in these filters.

These two filters will catch messages from non-AOL users without "real names":

when the message comes in or manual filtering is selected if From: matches regexp (case-insensitive) [a-z]$ unless   From: contains aol.com then Transfer To→z-ProbableJunkEmail, and Skip Rest
when the message comes in or manual filtering is selected if From: matches regexp ^< then Transfer To→z-ProbableJunkEmail and Skip Rest

Default Filter: I Don't Know You

If you don't get email from strangers regularly, you might want to put any message that gets to the end of the filter list into a separate mailbox. If you leave them in the inbox with no label, sorting by label will put them before all your other messages. If you move them to another mailbox, you might forget to look at that mailbox on a regular basis. Messages from unknown addresses are frequently junk, but sometimes the messages are important. For example, you don't want to miss a message from your mom telling you her new email address.

If your earlier filters stopped properly, only messages from strangers (or acquaintances who have changed their email addresses) will get to this filter.

Many of the headers will have periods in them. You can create a default action—regardless of the message's contents—by looking for a period in any of the headers.

Your default filter might look like this:

```
when the message comes in or manual filtering is selected
if «Any Header» contains .,
then Make Label→Unknown and Skip Rest
```

File Related Incoming and Outgoing Messages Together

Eudora can filter outgoing messages as well as incoming messages. This is handy if you want to keep both sides of a conversation together. For example, Mabel might want any messages to or from her husband to end up in her a-Charlie mailbox. She should have at least one filter for each label:

when a message goes out if «Any Recipient» contains charlie@electricbagpipes.com, then Transfer To→a-Charlie and Skip Rest
when a message goes out if «Any Recipient» intersects nickname MyFamily or   From: intersects nickname CharlieFamily, then Transfer To→b-Family and Skip Rest
when a message goes out if «Any Recipient» intersects nickname friends, then Transfer To→m-Friends and Skip Rest
when a message goes out if «Any Recipient» contains announce@flossrecycling.com then Transfer To→j-Announce, and Skip Rest
when a message goes out if «Any Recipient» intersects nickname payroll then Transfer To→h-Payroll and Skip Rest
when a message goes out if «Any Recipient» contains flossrecycling.com, then Transfer To→i-CoWorkers and Skip Rest

For a less-effective but simpler way to group incoming and outgoing messages together, see "How to Keep Conversations Together" on page 53.

Summary

- Filters work best with regular, predictable messages—like those from mailing lists—but many common messages are regular enough for you to filter.
- For messages that you group by label, you need to make two filters. Make one incoming filter to change the label and one manual filter to file the message.
- Unless a known spammer sent the message, you probably shouldn't delete junk email automatically. Instead, put it into a separate mailbox to look at later.
- Changing priority based on common keywords can be useful.
- Keeping related incoming and outgoing messages together can help you follow a conversation.

This chapter gives examples for filters that adjust the priority of messages, as well as ones that recognize and file messages:

CHAPTER 4

Move Around Your Messages Quickly

Eudora has a number of features that you can use to move through your messages more quickly. If you hate to take your hands off the keyboard, Eudora's many keyboard shortcuts can streamline your work. If you prefer to do everything with a mouse, adding new buttons to the toolbar can reduce the distance your mouse travels every day.

None of these shortcuts will give you an immediate, huge time savings. However, the number of messages that you get per year multiplied by the amount of time you save on each one works out to be a significant number. Just as importantly, these shortcuts can make reading email less tedious and give you a sense of control and competence.

This chapter focuses on shortcuts for moving through your messages. It covers

- ways to proceed quickly through your new messages
- how to add buttons to the toolbar
- how to quickly find and view a message or set of related messages
- how to quickly mark messages "done" or "to-do"
- where to look for further information on keyboard shortcuts

Move to the Next Message Easily

Probably the most common thing you do in Eudora is move to the next message. Saving even a little time on advancing to the next message can add up quickly.

How to Move to the Next Message with Keyboard Shortcuts

Bouncing back and forth from your keyboard to your mouse can get tedious, especially if you prefer to use the keyboard. One of the most common reasons people go to the mouse is to move to the next message. However, Eudora has very good keyboard shortcuts for moving to the next new message.

How to Move to the Next Message with Arrow Keys

Pressing the arrow keys with a modifier key moves you from message to message. Eudora for Windows's default modifier key is Alt. Alt-↑ and Alt-← open the previous message; Alt-↓ and Alt-→ open the next message.

If you don't like Alt, you can select a different modifier key. Select Tools→Options...→ Miscellaneous. Next, check one of the boxes in the section titled Switch Messages with, as indicated by the arrow in Figure 24:

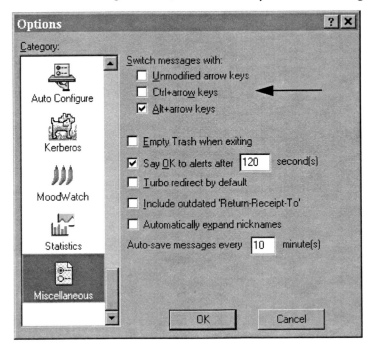

Figure 24: Setting Modifier Key for Arrow Keys (Windows)

The Mac OS modifier key is normally Command. If you haven't changed the settings, typing Command-↑ or Command-← opens the previous message and Command-↓ or Command-→ opens the next message. To change the modifier key, go to Special→Settings→Moving Around and select a different checkbox in the section labeled Arrow+these modifiers to switch messages, as shown by the arrow in Figure 25.

You might be tempted to use the arrow keys without a modifier key. Unfortunately, if you are using Mac OS and change the setting so that you don't need a modifier key to switch messages, you won't be able to use the arrow keys when editing messages.

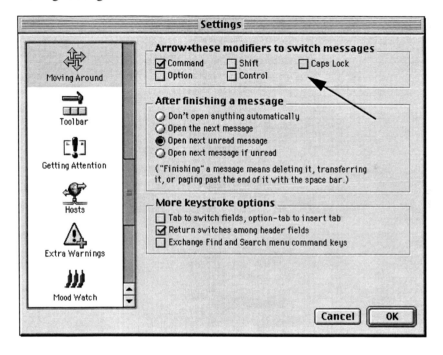

Figure 25: Setting Modifier Key for Arrow Keys (Mac OS)

How to Move to the Next Message with the Space Bar

In addition to switching messages with the arrow keys, you can move quickly through messages with the Space bar. If you have selected a message in a mailbox, Space can open the message in its own window.

If the message is long enough that it doesn't all fit in the window, Space can scroll the message down one page. If you're at the end of a message, Space can open the next message. Thus hitting the biggest key on the keyboard repeatedly can take you through the entire text of all your messages.

Mac OS Eudora normally has this behavior. Windows Eudora, however, does something different by default. To make the space bar take you to the next message, select Tools→Options…→Viewing Mail. Uncheck the box next to Use Microsoft's viewer and make sure there is a check mark in the box labeled Automatically open next message. Your settings should look similar to the window in Figure 26:

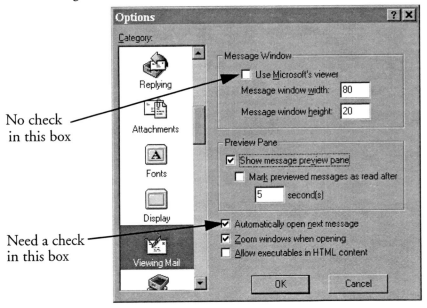

Figure 26: (Don't) Use Microsoft's viewer (Windows only)

There is a disadvantage to unchecking the Use Microsoft's viewer box. Some messages with styled text are a little bit prettier when displayed with Microsoft's viewer than with Eudora's built-in viewer. However, if you are keyboard-oriented, being able to use the spacebar to move through messages is probably more valuable than slightly better looking messages.

Space Takes You Where?

If you have configured Windows as discussed in the previous section, `Space` opens the next message in its own window.

With Mac OS, you can set what you want to happen when you are at the end of a message and hit `Space`. By default, Eudora opens the next *unread* message instead of the next message. This is a very useful behavior: usually you don't want to see messages you've already read.

However, you might want to switch temporarily to move to the next message—read *or* unread—if you need to hunt through a large block of old messages. To do this, change the `After finishing a message` setting in `Special`→`Settings...`→`Moving Around` (shown in Figure 25).

Note that "next unread message" really means "next unread message as sorted in this mailbox." For example, suppose that you go through three messages in the same order that they are sorted in the mailbox. If you read one message, skip one, and then read the last one, then there will not be a "next unread message." The one that you skipped is "*before*"— not "next" after—the message you just finished.

If you have unread messages in a different mailbox, you will need to make that mailbox active before you can move to the "next unread" message in that mailbox.

How to Move to the Next Message by Filtering

As discussed in "Separate 'To-Do' Messages from 'Done' Messages" on page 47, if you prioritize with labels and filter your messages after you read them, you can move through your messages very quickly by alternating between "show the next message" and "manually filter" commands:

- If you are keyboard-oriented, press `Command-j` if you are done with a message and `Space` if you are not.
- If you are mouse-oriented, you can be just as fast by putting two buttons in your toolbar: one for filtering and one for moving to the next message. (An explanation of how to add buttons is coming up soon in "How to Put Buttons in the Toolbar" on page 95.)

- If you don't want to put any more buttons in your toolbar, you can filter by the menu command Special→Filter Messages. There is no menu option to move to the next message.

Eudora's exact behavior after filtering a message depends on whether you are using Eudora for Windows or Eudora for Mac OS and whether the Message Preview Pane is open, as shown in Figure 27:

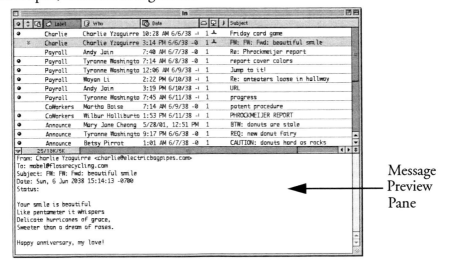

Message Preview Pane

Figure 27: Message Preview Pane

If the Message Preview Pane is open, Eudora replaces the message in the Message Preview Pane with the next message when you manually filter the current message into another mailbox.

If you are looking at a message in its own window and you manually filter that message, Eudora will first close that message. Eudora for Mac OS will open the next unread message in its own window. Eudora for Windows will not open a new message.

Therefore, if you use Eudora for Windows, you will need to read messages in the Message Preview Pane for this organizing strategy to work well.

How to Move to Next Message by Transferring It to a Mailbox

If you are using Eudora for Windows, you can transfer a message to another mailbox by pressing Alt-r. This will bring up the Transfer menu. Then, typing the first letter(s) of a mailbox will move the message into that mailbox. This is useful for transferring "to-do" messages in your medium priority mailboxes into the inbox, as discussed on page 48.

Using Eudora for Windows, if you read a message in the message Message Preview Pane, transferring the message will make the Message Preview Pane show the next message. If the message is open in its own window, transferring it will only close the window. Again, if you are using Windows, you probably want to use the Message Preview Pane.

If you use Mac OS, transferring a message to another mailbox will cause the next unread message to appear, regardless of whether you're reading the message in the Message Preview Pane or in its own window. (Note that Eudora for Mac OS doesn't have a keyboard shortcut for transferring a message. You either have to transfer it with a menu command, by dragging it to a mailbox, or with a button in the toolbar.)

How to Put Buttons in the Toolbar

If you are using Paid or Sponsored mode, you can customize your toolbar. If there are menu operations or keystrokes that you do frequently, turning them into one-click operations can save you time. For example, if you prefer the mouse to the keyboar and use Eudora for Mac OS (which doesn't have built-in toolbar buttons for moving to the next message), you might like to add a button for Command-↓.

You can even use menu commands that are not built in. For example, if you save a search, that search becomes a menu item. You then can add a button to the toolbar to run that search. ("How to Find Related Messages Over and Over (Mac OS only)" on page 105 shows how to save searches.)

You need to do different things under Mac OS and Windows to add, remove, and replace buttons.

How to Make Toolbar Buttons with Eudora for Mac OS

To change a button with Eudora for Mac OS, Command-click on one of the toolbar buttons. A dialog box like the one in Figure 28 will appear:

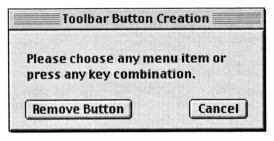

Figure 28: Modify Toolbar Button Dialog Box (Mac OS)

You can select any menu action or press any keyboard shortcut (like Command-↓). Eudora will then put a button for that action in the toolbar.

To add a new button, do the same thing you would to change a button, but Command-click on the line between two existing buttons.

To remove a button, Command-click on the button, then click on Remove Button in the dialog box (as seen in Figure 28).

How to Make Toolbar Buttons with Eudora for Windows

If you are using Windows, **to add a toolbar button**, you need to right-click on the toolbar, then select Customize.... A window like the one in Figure 29 will appear.

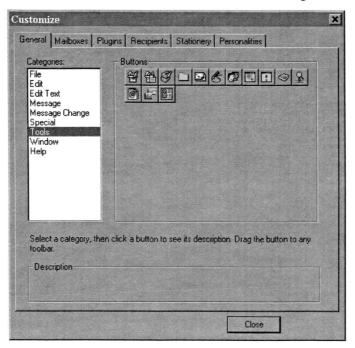

Figure 29: Customize Toolbar Window (Windows)

There are so many different actions that a button could take that they are divided into general categories by the tabs along the top, then into smaller categories by the vertical list on the left-hand side of the window. The pictures on the right are what the button will actually look like in the toolbar.

Unfortunately, you can't tell immediately what each picture corresponds to. You need to select an icon to see its description. The description will then appear in the box at the bottom of the window.

Once you have decided on an action, drag its icon to the toolbar and Close the Customize Toolbar window.

To move a toolbar button to a different place on the toolbar, hold the `Alt` key while dragging the button to its new location. **To remove a toolbar button**, hold the `Alt` key while dragging the button off the toolbar.

Quickly Mark Messages "Done" or "To-Do"

I believe that moving messages out of the inbox by filtering (as discussed in "Separate 'To-Do' Messages from 'Done' Messages" on page 47) is the most efficient way to mark messages "done." If you agree, you can skip to "How to Find Messages" on page 100.

If you want to know what other options you have, keep reading. If you don't have Eudora and are only reading this book because I haven't written a book for your email program yet, keep reading.

(Don't) Mark Messages Done by Deleting

Some people delete each message as soon as they finish with it. This makes seeing to-do items easy: the inbox has to-do items and nothing else. However, this means they can't refer to old messages to help them:

- **remember important facts:** "Who replaced Winston?" or "What did the VP say the third quarter's financial goals were?"
- **train others:** "What have been the major issues in the department recently?"
- **prove that they did something:** "Did I submit all of my status reports on time?" Some people even send themselves messages in order to have a dated record of a thought they had or an action they took.

Deleting all messages when you are done with them is like deliberately losing your memory. Imagine if you threw out all of the papers in your filing cabinet every month!

If you delete some things but not others, you have to take some time to decide what to keep and what to throw away. This might only take a tiny bit of time, but it adds up when you do it over and over again. It is faster to keep everything.

It also probably isn't worth your time to periodically purge your files in hopes of finding old messages more quickly in the future. Find and Search work so well and so quickly that cleaning out old messages probably won't save as much time as it takes.

Disk space was once expensive. It was not economically possible to keep all of your email messages. But now, text messages are now ridiculously small compared to the size of hard disks. You probably won't ever need to throw away text messages. (Attachments are different. Attachments are often big enough that you may need to clean out your attachments directory periodically.)

Mark "To-Do" Messages Unread

One way to mark your "to-do" messages is to make them Unread. Mailboxes with unread messages will be underlined (Mac OS) or bold (Windows) in the mailboxes window.

You can put a button in the toolbar for marking a message Unread. If you are using Eudora for Windows, you can switch a message's status quickly between Read and Unread by pressing Shift-Space. Eudora for Mac OS does not have a keyboard shortcut.

If you are using Mac OS, you can save a search that will show you all of your unread messages, sorted by mailbox. Saving searches is covered in "How to Find Related Messages Over and Over (Mac OS only)" on page 105.

Open "To-Do" Messages in Their Own Windows

When you close Eudora, it remembers where your windows are and reopens them when you restart Eudora. That means that you can mark a "to-do" message by opening it in its own window and leaving the window open until you have finished with the message. You can then see at a glance how many messages you need to deal with.

You could even choose to use your filters to open your high-priority messages in their own window, as discussed on page 50. Eudora opens messages on the left-hand side of the screen, so moving "to-do" windows to the right-hand side of your screen is an easy way to separate new messages and old "to-do" messages.

You can then mark messages "done" just by closing them. To close a window, click in the close box or press Command-w (Mac OS) or Control-w (Windows). (Don't worry that Eudora will close the messages when you quit the program. When you re-start, Eudora will re-open any windows that were open when you quit.)

Mac OS users will probably like this technique more than Windows users. Eudora for Mac OS has a transparent background, while the Windows version has a gray background. If you make the Eudora for Windows window large enough for all your messages, you'll have trouble seeing other programs. The title bar on Mac OS windows also takes less room than title bars under Windows.

If you need more room on your screen, you can minimize (Windows) or roll up (Mac OS) the message window. You can also reduce the size of your windows with the techniques you will learn in "How to Make More Room on Your Monitor" on page 105.

You might be concerned that you'll end up with too many open windows to manage. This certainly can be a problem, but you probably won't have as many windows open as you think. Only a small fraction of your new messages will turn into "to-do" items. You might only have a few open messages and a few open mailboxes under normal circumstances.

TIP: Go through your filters and disable window opening before you download a large number of new messages. If you have a thousand new messages, that can lead to hundreds of windows opening. You probably don't want to wait for so many windows to open. (Your computer might even crash if it tries to open too many windows.)

How to Find Messages

A message that you can't find is just as gone as a message you deleted. Fortunately, Eudora has simple but powerful features for finding messages. I assume you're already familiar with the Special/Edit→Find→Search tool, which is pretty easy to find and figure out. There are a number of ways to find messages that are not as obvious or intuitive. This section will describe different ways to find messages.

If you are sure that you are familiar with all the possible ways to find messages, you can skip to "Move to the Next Message Easily" on page 89. However, Eudora has many little tricks that are not obvious. I recommend reading this section.

How to Sort Mailboxes

As mentioned briefly in "Group by Category" on page 30, Eudora can rearrange mailboxes in many different ways. This can help you find messages faster.

Clicking on any mailbox's column header sorts all the messages in that mailbox by that column. For example, clicking on Subject sorts all the messages alphabetically from A to Z by subject.

Holding Option (Mac OS) or Shift (Windows) down while clicking on a heading does a *reverse* sort. For example, if you Option-click/Shift-click on Subject, Eudora will sort all the messages from Z to A by subject.

Eudora can also sort by multiple columns. If you are using Eudora for Windows, hold down the Control key and click on several columns one after another. Eudora will sub-sort the messages, with the first column clicked being most important and the last column clicked being least important. For example, suppose you Control-click on Who, then Subject, then Date. Eudora will group each correspondent's messages together. For each correspondent, all the messages will be sorted by subject. For each correspondent and subject, the messages will be sorted by date.

Eudora for Windows puts a little triangle in the header of the column that the mailbox is sorted by. If you've sorted the mailbox by multiple columns, all of the sort columns will have little triangles, with a tiny number inside that tells what that column's sort order is. For example, look at the triangles indicated by the arrows in Figure 30. They show that this mailbox is sorted first by Label, second by Date, and third by Subject:

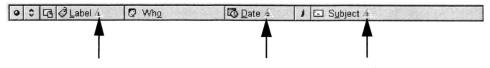

Figure 30: Mailbox Column Headers (Windows)

If you are using Eudora for Mac OS, you don't have to hold a key down to sort by multiple columns, but you have to click on the column headers in the reverse order from Windows. For example, suppose you want the same effect as mentioned in earlier: each correspondent's messages grouped together, then sorted by subject, then by date. You need to click on Date first, then Subject, then Who.

TIP: Eudora ignores Re: and Fwd: when sorting mailboxes by subject.

How to Sort by Read/Unread Status

You might be tempted to separate all the Read messages from the Unread messages by sorting on Read (the column with the little blue ball at the top). This works reasonably well for Windows, but not for Mac OS.

Under Mac OS, as soon as you open a message, Eudora changes its status to Read and moves the message to the Read section of the list. If you try to move to the "next" message, Eudora will take you to a message that you have already read!

How to Find Messages in a Mailbox by Typing

If you type something while a mailbox is the active window, Eudora shows the message with the Who or Subject entry that is alphabetically closest to what you typed. (Eudora uses the Who column unless you have sorted by Subject.) For example, if you sort by subject and type t, the mailbox will change to highlight a message whose Subject starts with T. If no messages start with T, Eudora will highlight the message with the subject line that starts with the letter closest to T.

If you type quickly enough, Eudora looks for a whole word. For example, you could type inter if you wanted to find all messages with the subject of interview candidate instead of messages with subject of Italian distributor or icky smell in cafeteria. However, if you pause for too long between letters, Eudora starts a new search with the next letter. For example, if you pause between int and er, you might end up looking at a message with the subject erase my hard drive?!?!

If the mailbox is not sorted by Subject, Eudora starts by looking for the letters that you typed in first names. If there are no first names with those letters, it then looks for the letters in the last (second) name. For example, suppose your inbox has messages from

- Andy Jain
- Chantelle Williams
- Claire Beekman
- Jeff Chee
- Loretta Garcia
- Alicia Vandeschaf
- Tyrone Washington
- Wayan Li

If you type j in your inbox, Eudora will highlight a message from Jeff Chee. If you type ja (quickly), Eudora will highlight a message from Andy Jain.

How to Show Related Messages

Eudora can help you find related messages. If you Option-click (Mac OS) or Alt-click (Windows) on a message line in a mailbox window, then Eudora will reorder the mailbox to bring together and highlight all the messages with the same contents as the column you clicked on. To restore the normal order, just click on one of the column headers.

If Mabel Option/Alt-clicks on Tyronne Washington, Eudora will highlight and group all messages from Tyronne that are in the mailbox, as seen in Figure 31:

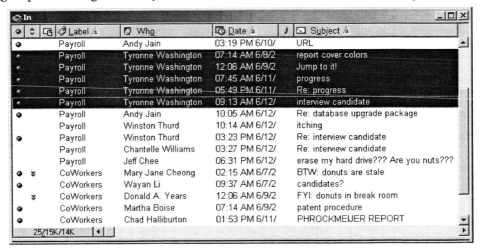

Figure 31: Show Messages From Tyronne (Windows)

If Mabel Option/Alt-clicks on interview candidate instead, Eudora will group all messages with the subject interview candidate or Re: interview candidate. as shown in Figure 32:

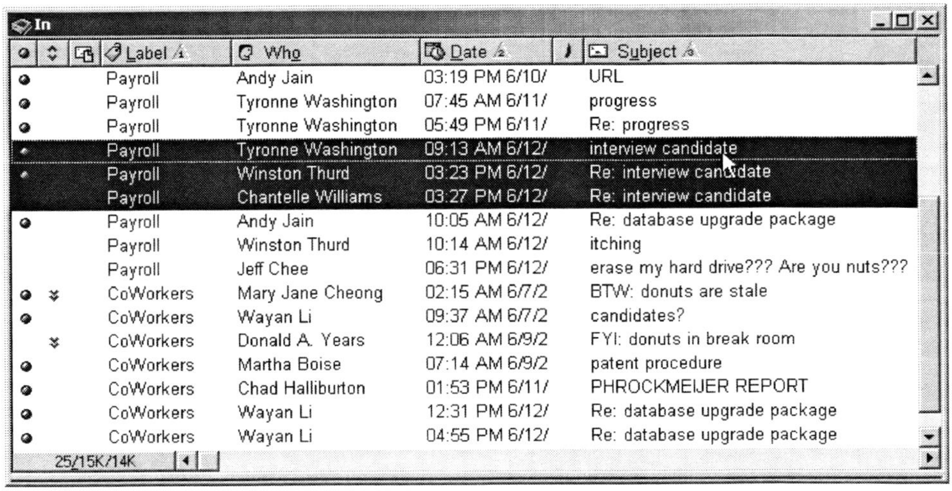

Figure 32: Interview Candidate Messages (Windows)

This technique works extremely well. Typing the name or subject that you are looking for, then Option/Alt-clicking on the name or subject is much faster than doing a Special/Edit→Find→Search. I find myself using Option/Alt-click many times each day.

How to Find Related Messages Over and Over (Mac OS only)

If you are using Mac OS, you can save a search to use over and over again. Select Special→Find→Search and set up the search that you want. Then select File→Save As and give that search a name. You can then run that search at any time by selecting Special→Find→*(name of your search)* and then clicking on the Search button.

For example, you might create a search to find all unread messages in mailboxes other than Out, Trash, and z-ProbableJunkEmail. If you name it Unread, then you can run that search at any time by selecting Special→Find→Unread, then clicking on the Search button. (And now that you've got a menu action for it, you can make a toolbar button for it.)

How to Make More Room on Your Monitor

You can keep track of your messages more easily if you can see them all. Eudora displays many pieces of information that you might not need to see. Hiding that information will give you more room on your monitor for information you care about.

Make More Room by Closing the Mailboxes Window

If you have a lot of windows open, you might want to save space on the screen by closing the Mailboxes Window. You can always see the list of mailboxes quickly by pulling down the Mailbox menu.

Mailboxes with unread messages are underlined (Mac OS) or have a little envelope icon next to them (Windows) in the Mailbox menu.

Make More Room by Closing the Message Preview Pane

If all of a group's messages are in their own windows, you don't need to see a preview of it. You might want to close the Message Preview Pane in some or all of your mailboxes to give you more room on the screen. With Mac OS, to close the Message Preview Pane, click on the triangle at the left of the strip between the list of messages and the Message Preview Pane, as indicated by the arrow in Figure 33:

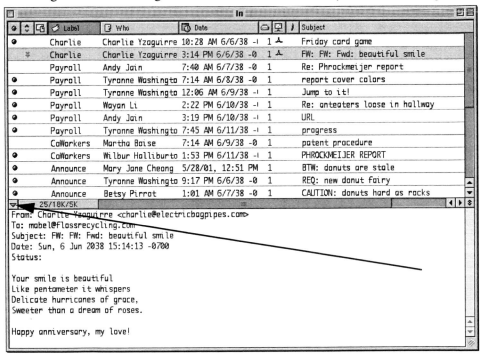

Figure 33: Close Message Preview Pane (Mac OS)

While Mac OS users can open and close the Message Preview Pane on a mailbox-by-mailbox basis, Windows users must either open or close *all* Message Preview Panes together. Windows users need to select Tools→Options…, then select the Viewing Mail window. Uncheck the box next to Show message preview pane.

Make More Room by Hiding Columns

Eudora normally shows many columns in mailbox windows. You probably don't need to see all of the columns. For example, once you become familiar with the color-coding of your labels, you probably don't need to see the Label column. You might also find that you never look at the Size, Server, and Mood (Mac OS) columns or the Size, Server Status, and Mood Watch (Windows) columns.

You can control which columns appear by selecting Special→Settings…→ Mailbox Display (Mac OS) or Tools→Options…→Mailboxes (Windows) and unchecking the boxes next to columns you don't care about, as shown by the arrow in Figure 34:

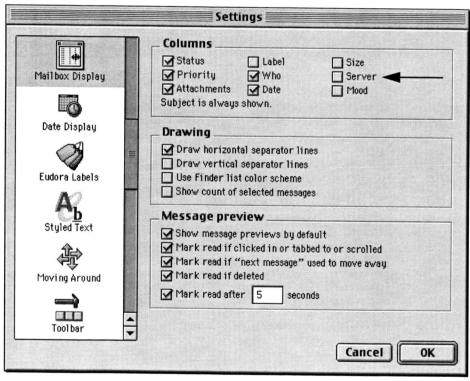

Figure 34: Control Mailbox Column Display (Mac OS)

More Keyboard Shortcuts

There are many more shortcuts in Eudora than I covered in this chapter. I cover more in later chapters, but you might want to look quickly through the others. To see a list of all of the keyboard shortcuts, select Help→Modifiers and Shortcuts (Mac OS) or Help→Modifiers→Index and type in keyboard shortcuts (Windows).

Summary

- The arrow keys (with a modifier key) can take you quickly through messages.
- The Space bar can take you quickly through messages. If you're using Windows, you might need to uncheck the box in Tools→Options…→ Miscellaneous labeled Use Microsoft's Viewer.
- You can mark messages by transferring them out of the inbox, opening them in their own windows, or marking them Unread. Deleting messages to show that you are done with them is fast but prevents you from using old messages.
- Eudora's exact behavior on filtering or transferring a message depends upon whether the message is in the Message Preview Pane or its own window and on which operating system you are using.
- You can save time by adding toolbar buttons for Eudora operations that you do frequently.
- You can reduce the size of your mailboxes by closing the Message Preview Pane and removing some columns from the display.
- Eudora has powerful features for finding messages, including:
  - the Special/Edit→Find→Search tool
  - sorting a mailbox by column(s)
  - showing all related messages that are in the same mailbox
- If you are using Eudora for Mac OS, you can save common searches for re-use.

Reduce the Number of Incoming Messages

Organizing and prioritizing messages helps decrease the amount of time you spend on email, but reducing the number of incoming messages can save you even more time. Obviously, you want some of your email, but some messages are unnecessary. Junk email is one form of unnecessary email, but even non-junk messages can waste your time.

For example, mailing lists, while useful, can generate an enormous amount of traffic. Off-topic postings, arguments, and just plain boring mailing list messages waste your time.

Sometimes, email from strangers doesn't waste as much time as messages from people you know. After all, you can figure out very quickly if a message is junk email. You might even be able to use filters to get rid of it, as shown in "File Junk" on page 77. On the other hand, you might need to read all messages from your boss through to the end.

This chapter shows how to reduce the number of these three types of messages: junk email, mailing lists, and nuisance messages from acquaintances. Some of the techniques require some extra effort at first but will save you time in the end.

Reduce the Number of Junk Email Messages

Junk email is very annoying. If you don't get junk email now, consider yourself lucky—and take steps to make sure you don't *start* getting junk email. If you already get junk email, you might want to start over with a new email account, then keep that account away from junk emailers.

Your company's Information Technology department might have a way of getting rid of junk email before it ever gets to your mailbox, saving you download time. You might need to ask for the service, however. Find your company's email system administrator and ask, "Can I get a spam filter on my account?"

The best thing you can do to keep from getting junk email is keep your email address private. Don't put your email address on a Web page, don't put messages up on any of the public Internet discussion forums, and don't give your email address out to retailers.

TIP: This is such an important point that I will repeat it to make sure you see it: **Keep your work email address private!!**

If keeping your email address private would interfere too much with your use of the Internet (or if your email address is already on junk email lists), consider getting a second email account. As mentioned in "Use Multiple Accounts to Group Messages" on page 57, there are now a number of services that will give you free accounts. You can use one account for public contact and one for private contact, effectively separating your email into two groups: junk and non-junk.

Reduce the Number of Mailing List Messages

Mailing lists are a great way to communicate with people who have shared interests and goals. However, they can lead to an enormous amount of email traffic. Filters can help enormously by grouping messages from a mailing list into their own mailbox, but that might not be enough. Fortunately, there are a few things you can do to save time with mailing lists.

Mailing List Administration

Before reading more about mailing lists, you need to understand that a piece of software—not a human being—administers most mailing lists. This software (called a *list server, listserv,* or *listbot*) allows people to join or leave the list without causing work for anybody else. Yes, there is a human being—the *list owner*—who has control over the list server, but he or she is not guaranteed to pay any attention to the list server. The list owner might not even read the list messages. It is thus important to know how to communicate with the list server.

When you join or *subscribe* to a list, the first message usually gives instructions for how to communicate with the list server. It will tell you what options you have and what the list server's email address is. (Usually the list server's address is different from the address you use to reach subscribers. The subscribers are reached by the *listname address*.)

Be sure to save that first message in a safe place. If you occasionally delete large blocks of old messages, be sure to move that first message into a special mailbox that you don't ever delete. (I put mine in a mailbox with other confirmation messages from automated services.)

If you subscribed to a mailing list by sending an email message, the most important thing to remember is the list server's email address. Putting the list server's email address into your address book will help you find it in the future.

If you subscribed to a mailing list from a Web page, the most important thing to remember is where that Web page is. That page should take you to information about how to communicate with the list server. You should send yourself email with the location of the Web page and file that message someplace safe. (You could bookmark it in your Web browser, but if you have lots of bookmarks, you might have a hard time finding it.)

When to Unsubscribe

There are several situations where you should unsubscribe from your mailing lists:

- If your email takes up too much of your time, ask yourself if you really need to be on all your mailing lists. In particular, if the list has an archive on a Web site, you might want to look at the archive occasionally instead of letting messages from the list fill a mailbox.
- When you go on vacation, you might want to temporarily unsubscribe. You will probably want to spend your first day back from vacation going through only your hundreds of work-related messages, not also your hundreds of mailing list messages.
- You should unsubscribe when you change email addresses. Unsubscribe using your old address and resubscribe with your new address. Many list servers look at the return address to decide whether to honor a removal request. If your return address has changed since you subscribed, the list server might not honor your requests. (This is an appropriate security feature. You don't really want your worst enemy to alter your mailing list subscriptions, do you?)

  If all the email from your old account is forwarded to the new account, you could be stuck with the mailing list forever.

How to Unsubscribe

How to unsubscribe from a mailing list is not as obvious as you would hope. There are many different kinds of list servers, each with a slightly different set of commands. This is why you should save the instructions! Three years from now, you might want to unsubscribe and not remember how.

You could be lucky: list servers frequently put unsubscribe instructions in every message. For example, all messages that go through Yahoo Groups currently have a header with the unsubscribe address, like this:

```
List-Unsubscribe: <mailto:moo-unsubscribe@yahoogroups.com>
```

Other Internet distribution lists frequently add unsubscribe instructions at the end of the message. Some others put the unsubscribe address in a header. Look at the top and bottom of recent messages before doing anything else.

Get Help from the List Server

If you have lost the original instructions but still have the list server's address, first try getting help from the list server. Commands like `info` and `help` followed by the name of the list might get you more information. Nonsense like `slkdfj` might also convince the list server that you need help. A message like this will probably get *something* useful in response:

```
To: lists@catfloss.org
Subject: help floss-talk

help floss-talk
info floss-talk
alsdjfaj floss-talk
```

If nothing else, the response will probably tell you the correct way to ask the list server for information.

If that doesn't tell you how to unsubscribe, you can try a few of the common ways to unsubscribe. Usually you unsubscribe by putting one of the following key words in the body and/or the subject header of a message to the list server:

```
unsubscribe
remove
leave
```

Sometimes you need to put your email address after the name of the list. For example:

```
To: lists@catfloss.org
Subject: unsubscribe floss-talk

unsubscribe floss-talk mabel@flossrecycling.com
```

Try several different unsubscribe messages. After no more than three or four tries, you'll probably succeed in either unsubscribing or getting directions on how to unsubscribe.

How Not to Unsubscribe

As mentioned earlier, the list server has a different address than the listname address, so sending a removal request to the list name address usually does nothing except make you look really stupid. Not only are "please remove me" messages a way to lower people's opinion of your intelligence, but you might also get swamped with incoming messages. Fifty people might explain the proper way to unsubscribe—and they might not all be polite.

If you can't remember how to unsubscribe from a mailing list and have misplaced the instructions, at least apologize if you ask the list subscribers how to unsubscribe. You might still look like an idiot, but you will at least look like a *polite* idiot.

I am on a mailing list where instructions on how to unsubscribe are at the bottom of *every* message. People get really annoyed when they see messages like this:

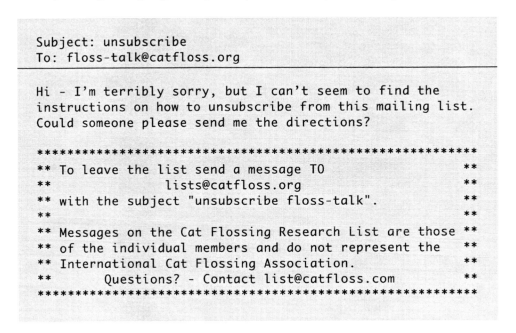

```
Subject: unsubscribe
To: floss-talk@catfloss.org
───────────────────────────────────────────────────────
Hi - I'm terribly sorry, but I can't seem to find the
instructions on how to unsubscribe from this mailing list.
Could someone please send me the directions?

**********************************************************
**  To leave the list send a message TO              **
**              lists@catfloss.org                   **
**  with the subject "unsubscribe floss-talk".        **
**                                                   **
**  Messages on the Cat Flossing Research List are those **
**  of the individual members and do not represent the  **
**  International Cat Flossing Association.           **
**        Questions? - Contact list@catfloss.com      **
**********************************************************
```

Switch to Mailing List Digests

If you get a lot of messages from a mailing list, you might want to get the messages in a *digest*—a single email message that combines all the messages sent to the list in one day or one week. Getting a digest won't reduce the amount of text that you have to read, but it might make the messages easier to deal with. If you can't restrain yourself from reading *any* message when it appears in your inbox, this might keep your day from getting too fragmented.

Unfortunately, there are three potential disadvantages to digests:

- Digests are very long, so they require a lot of scrolling.
- It is harder to reply to the author of one of the messages in the digest. (Selecting "reply" will send a reply to either the entire list or to nobody.) You'll need to copy and paste the author's address into a new message's To: header.
- You can't skip individual messages as easily.

With some, but not all, digests, Eudora for Mac OS can *burst* them—split them into their individual messages. You need to put a checkmark in the box in Special→Settings…→Attachments next to Receive MIME digests as attachments. Some digest messages will then appear as attachments. Double-clicking on the attachment will put all the messages from that digest into their own mailbox, creating the mailbox if needed.

As I mentioned earlier, this doesn't work for all digests. This isn't exactly Eudora's fault: different mailing list programs can (and do) assemble digests in different ways. There are, however, a few Eudora plug-ins that recognize more forms of digests than Eudora does. See

http://www.OvercomeEmailOverload.com/eudora/tech.html

Switch to Announcement-Only Mailing Lists

If you want to stay informed of only the most important aspects of a topic, you might want to see if you can subscribe to an *announcements* list. Sometimes, interest groups will have two mailing lists for a particular topic: one for announcements only and one for general discussion. Announcement lists generally have many fewer messages than general discussion lists.

TIP: Sometimes, the names of announcement lists end in -announce and the discussion lists end in -talk. Digests frequently end in -digest. For example, roses-talk@rosegardens.org is almost certain to be a general discussion list.

Switch to Moderated Mailing Lists

If a lot of the messages on a list are not useful—idiots ranting, chain letters, messages that are off-topic, and so on—you might want to switch to one with some human quality control. On some lists, a human being (called a *moderator*) reads each of the messages and decides whether or not to let the message go to everyone who is subscribed. While the moderator might distribute guidelines for what he or she considers appropriate, in the end the moderator gets to decide what goes through. Because of the moderator, you won't have complete freedom of expression, but the percentage of useful messages should be higher than in an unmoderated list.

There won't always be a moderated list on the topic that interests you. If you'd like to provide a useful public service, you could volunteer to moderate a mailing list.

Reduce the Number of Messages from Acquaintances

Mailing lists can generate many messages, but you can usually wait to read and respond to them. Messages from friends and colleagues, however, need more careful attention. Reducing the number of those messages might help you more than getting rid of mailing list messages.

Write to Discourage Responses

There are a number of techniques you can use when writing messages that will make your correspondents less motivated to respond. These include

- sending clear messages
- writing with formality
- making clear that you think the conversation is over
- keeping your thanks until later
- avoiding rhetorical questions

Write with Formality

You can affect how many responses you get to your email messages by changing how formal your writing is. People naturally use very formal language to recognize that the audience can't respond easily. For example, here are three situations where people use very formal language. In each, there is a barrier to communicating freely:

- **When addressing people with radically different status.** If you and the Ambassador have tea, one of you might ask about the other's health, but both of you are socially constrained from actually discussing recent surgeries. The formal language you would use with the Ambassador reflects those social constraints.
- **When addressing an audience of the future.** Politicians know that lawyers might examine their documents carefully decades or even centuries later. The original authors might not be alive then to answer questions. The formal language in legal documents is a way of showing that nobody will be able to answer questions later.
- **When addressing a large number of people.** If every member of a large audience tried to comment on a speech, there would be chaos. The audience is not completely free to respond. The formal language used in speeches encourages people not to interrupt.

Intimate discussions, on the other hand, use very informal language. If you were as formal with your loved ones as with the Ambassador, they would probably wonder why you were angry! Advertisements use informal language deliberately to try to make the message seem more intimate (and therefore more trustworthy).

So be cautious about your messages' tone. If you want people to respond, be chatty and informal. If you want to discourage people from responding, send messages that are more formal.

Send Clear Messages

If your correspondents misunderstand your message, they will have to send you messages asking for clarification. You'll have to read at least one more message and write at least one more message.

Writing more understandable email is such a large and important topic that it's split into several chapters: Chapter 7, *Reduce Ambiguity*, Chapter 8, *Convey Emotional Tone*, and Chapter 9, *Make Messages Legible*.

Use "No Reply Needed"

Email doesn't have clear and common conventions for how to end a conversation, unlike in verbal conversations. In person, body language can say, "I'm leaving now." On the telephone, people say, "goodbye" to signal the end of the call. Email is new enough that conventions to end the conversation haven't developed yet.

You can help create a new standard. I recommend showing that the conversation is at an end by saying No Reply Needed. (Why did I capitalize No Reply Needed? Because I hope that someday people will abbreviate it NRN.)

For example:

```
Subject: Re: Phrockmeijer report

Alicia -

The Phrockmeijer report is on-line at
    http://internal.flossrecycling.com/~mabel/phrock.pdf

No Reply Needed.

--
Mabel
```

If you put FYI in the Subject: header, that will also show that you don't need a response. Use No Reply Needed when you are pretty sure that the receiver wants the information; use FYI when you aren't sure.

Don't Thank Your Correspondents Right Away

"Thank you" and "You're welcome" are particularly uninteresting closing comments. In spoken conversations, they are in context and very brief. They are polite, gracious, and make interactions more pleasant. However, in an email conversation, it might take you a moment to figure out what a message that just says "thank you" is about.

You can discourage messages that only say, "You're welcome" by not sending messages that only say, "Thank you." If you have a question about the favor, thank your correspondent when asking your question:

Subject: Re: Phrockmeijer report

Mabel -

Thanks a bunch for telling me so promptly where I could find the report.

I'm confused about one thing, though. The report says that the floss is green. Didn't we switch to purple three weeks ago?

--
Alicia

But unless it was an exceptional effort to get you the information, do your correspondent a favor and wait until your next message to say thanks:

Subject: Floss Expo

Mabel -

Thanks for getting me the Phrockmeijer report last week.

Jose reminded me that Floss Expo is coming up soon. Can you spare some Payroll clerks to staff the booths again?

--
Alicia

Another thing you can do is gives thanks profusely in advance:

```
Subject: Re: Floss Expo

Alicia -

Yes, I think Winston and Jeff would like to work Floss Expo
again. I'll ask them.

In the meantime, could you email me the latest version of
our brochures so they can get up to speed?

Thanks in advance!
--
Mabel
```

While I don't recommend it, some people abbreviate Thanks In Advance to TIA;
I've also seen advTHANKSance—the word "thanks" in(side) the word "advance."

Some people don't like thanking in advance. They feel that it is rude to assume
that the receiver will do the favor. I agree, it is—but so is not thanking someone
and so is contributing to someone's email overload by sending them messages that
just say "thank you".

Avoid Rhetorical Questions

Some questions are rhetorical; you don't really want an answer. Unfortunately,
without verbal and gestural signals, it is hard for people to figure out when a
question is rhetorical. You're likely to get sincere answers to all your questions:

```
Subject: safes

> Claire --
> Have you ever seen those little safes in hotels? Please
> put some in the cafeteria for employees to keep their
> wallets and purses.

Yes, there was a safe in the closet of the hotel I stayed
in last week.
```

You're likely to get better responses if you reword your rhetorical questions as statements:

```
Subject: Re: safes

 Claire --

 Please put some small safes -- like the ones expensive
 hotels sometimes have -- in the cafeteria. I want employees
 to have a safe place for their wallets and purses.
```

Discourage Third-Party Discussions

Another good strategy for reducing the amount of incoming email is to discourage your correspondents from getting into conversations with each other.

Consider the following exchange:

- Alicia sends a message to Mabel, Jeff, and sixteen other people asking what color the brochure covers are.
- Mabel sends a message to Alicia, Jeff, and sixteen other people saying the covers are the same green as the new logo.
- Jeff sends a message to Mabel, Alicia, and the other sixteen saying that he hates the new logo.
- Jeff and Alicia send messages back and forth (Cc'ing the seventeen others) arguing about whether the new logo is better than the old one.
- Mabel and the sixteen others get annoyed at Alicia and Jeff's private argument pushing into their inboxes.

Granted, Jeff shouldn't have sent an off-topic message, but Mabel could have made it difficult for Alicia to see Jeff's message. Then Mabel (and the sixteen others) wouldn't have needed to read Alicia and Jeff's argument about the logo. This section will explain a few strategies for reducing conversations between your correspondents.

Reply to Sender Only

If Mabel had responded just to Alicia, then Jeff probably wouldn't have gotten involved in the conversation. Granted, Mabel wouldn't have had a chance to impress everyone else with her insight and wit, but perhaps that's just as well.

Being careful to respond only to the sender also can save you from the most common embarrassing email mistake: sending a message to more people than you intended. You've probably seen how dangerous this can be!

For example, suppose that Della accidentally replied to everybody—including Jessica—instead of just to Charlie with the following message.

```
To: Charlie Yzaguirre <charlie@electricbagpipes.com>,
    Jessica Robinson <jessica@electricbagpipes.com>,
    Mabel Garcia <mabel@flossrecycling.com>
From: Della.Hunt@electricbagpipes.com
Subject: Re: Friday card game

> Would you all be interested in getting together on Friday
> to play cards?

Charlie, you have got to be out of your mind to invite
Jessica to play cards. That woman cheats so much that I'm
amazed that she isn't in jail yet!
```

Reply-To-All mistakes can lead to, at best, a lot of messages telling you that you made a mistake. At worst, you'll make people angry and a *flame war*—an angry argument fought using email messages—could erupt. Either will eat up your time and energy.

Eudora can help you reply to the sender only. Select Special→Settings…→ Replying (Mac OS) or Tools→Options…→Replying (Windows). If you are using Mac OS, make sure that under Reply to All, the radio buttons next to When option key is down and Address Handling for Reply to All are checked. If you are using Windows, make sure that the box next to Map Ctrl-R to 'Reply to All' is *not* checked.

Use Bcc: Instead of To: or Cc:

Reducing the number of people you send a message to isn't always possible. A lot of people might need to read your message. However, you can use Bcc: to keep your correspondents from getting into discussions with each other due to Reply-To-All mistakes.

You might have already noticed that you can see all the addresses in the To: and Cc: headers, but can't see addresses in the Bcc: header. It's not that the sender's email program sends the Bcc: list to everyone, but the receiver's software *hides* it; the sender's email program never *sends* the list. Nobody can ever see the Bcc: list except the sender.

(Note: While it is normal for Bcc: addresses to be hidden, I have to admit that there do exist a few obscure email programs that transmit the Bcc: information. This is, however, *extremely* uncommon—I consider it a bug in those email programs. Eudora does not send the Bcc: list.)

You can probably see that Bcc: can significantly reduce the amount of follow-up discussion. Be careful, however: Bcc: has some dangers. In particular, it is easy for people on the Bcc: list to respond to everybody (except, of course, anyone on the Bcc: list) by mistake. This can have very embarrassing consequences if the original sender was supposed to keep the message secret!

For example, suppose Wilbur uses Bcc: to pass on a secret to Tyronne and Chris:

```
From: Wilbur Haliburton <wilbur@flossrecycling.com>,
To: Loy Duncan <loy@flossrecycling.com>
Bcc: Tyronne Washington <tyronne@flossrecycling.com>,
    Chris Olszewski <chris@flossrecycling.com>
Subject: Re: reference
```

```
Loy -

You may certainly use me as a job reference. I'm sorry
that you won't be staying with the company, but I can
understand that you want to move on.

Naturally, I will not tell anyone else about your leaving.


--
Wilbur
```

If Tyronne or Chris respond to everyone instead of just to Loy, Loy will learn that Wilbur didn't keep the secret. Loy would be very surprised to get this message from Chris:

```
From: Chris Olszewski <chris@flossrecycling.com>
To: Wilbur Haliburton <wilbur@flossrecycling.com>,
Loy Duncan <loy@flossrecycling.com>
Subject: Re: Interview
```

```
> You may certainly use me as a job reference. I'm sorry
> that you won't be staying with the company, but I can
> understand that you want to move on.

Wilbur, see if you can find out what Loy wants. If he needs
more money, we can probably arrange that. I'll go up to
$10K if I have to. We've gotten away with underpaying him
pretty horribly in the past.


--
Chris
```

(Note that Tyronne, who Wilbur also put in the Bcc: list, will not get this message.)

It is true that Chris is the one who made the mistake of replying to everyone instead of just to Wilbur. However, Chris couldn't have made that mistake if Wilbur had sent a separate copy instead of using Bcc:.

TIP: It is a bad idea to write down anything that you would be embarrassed for others to find out. Your co-workers might see the message over your shoulder. The receiver's co-workers might see the message on the receiver's screen. The receiver could even forward it to many people. You cannot completely control who sees your message.

If your correspondents filter messages based on whether the messages are addressed them specifically, putting their addresses in the Bcc: header might make their filters send your message into a low-priority mailbox.

How to Use Group Nicknames to Discourage Discussions

If you send a message to a group nickname that has a Full Name, your correspondents will only see the Full Name in your message, not all the addresses in the group nickname. For example, suppose that Mabel has a group nickname called honchos which has a Full Name of Hoopston Hollering Hangar Honchos. If Mabel sends a message to honchos, the receivers will see only Hoopston Hollering Hangar Honchos; in the To: header:

```
From: Mabel Garcia <mabel@flossrecycling.com>
To: Hoopston Hollering Hangar Honchos;
Subject: lost parachute

I can't find my parachute! Did anyone take it home after
the jump last Saturday (11 Jan)?
```

To give a Full Name to a group nickname, fill in the box labeled Full Name on the Personal tab in the Address Book, as shown by the arrow in Figure 35.

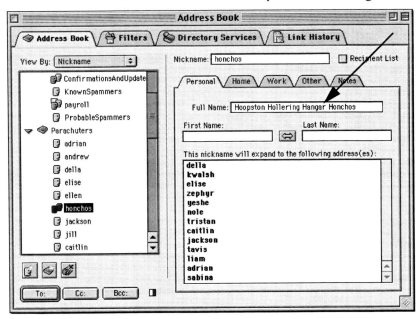

Figure 35: Adding Full Name to a Group Nickname (Mac OS)

If you sometimes want to show all the receivers, consider having two group nicknames, one with a Full Name and one without. For example, Mabel could have one nickname honchos with a blank Full Name and another nickname invisibleHonchos that has the Full Name of Hoopston Hollering Hangar Honchos. If Mabel sends a message to honchos, then all the names and email addresses will be visible in the messages people receive. If she sends to the invisibleHonchos list, no addresses will be visible.

(Mabel doesn't need to maintain two lists. When she creates invisibleHonchos, she can put just honchos in the box marked This nickname will expand to the following address(es). Adding someone to the honchos list will automatically add them to the invisibleHonchos list as well.)

Send Fewer Messages

One of the best ways to get fewer responses is to send fewer messages. This doesn't mean that you shouldn't send email at all. Email is a wonderful thing when used correctly! However, you should consider carefully whether your correspondents really want your message. In particular, be careful about sending anything to a large group of people. The more people who get a message, the more likely it is that someone will misinterpret the emotion, context, or meaning. You might need to read and send additional messages.

TIP: Before you send a message to a large group of people, consider whether you would go up to a microphone to say it to that many people in an auditorium. If you wouldn't say it in front of three hundred people, don't email it to three hundred people.

There are certain types of messages that will really annoy people. The more people you send such messages to, the more likely it is that you will get messages *back* that tell you not to do that. The rest of this section describes messages that you probably should not send.

"Me Too"

You might have already seen the "me too" message. This is fine when there are only two people in the discussion, but not when there are hundreds:

```
To: abuse-L@electricbagpipes.com
Subject: Re: junk email
From: newbie@electricbagpipes.com

Tyler Spratt <tspratt@electricbagpipes.com> said:
> I think that all people who waste Internet bandwidth
> should have their access cut off forever.

Me too!
```

You should only write your support to the entire recipient list if you have something new to add:

```
To: abuse-L@electricbagpipes.com
Subject: Re: junk email
From: newbie@electricbagpipes.com
───────────────────────────────────────────────────
Tyler Spratt <tspratt@electricbagpipes.com> said:
> I think that all people who waste Internet bandwidth
> should have their access cut off forever.

I agree in principle, but I think a permanent banishment
would be a bit extreme. Just take our... uh... *their* Web
connection away for a week. That will teach them!
```

Otherwise, keep quiet. The second, third, and seventy-third identical "me too" messages aren't interesting.

Sometimes, someone on a mailing list will ask for your opinion or vote. In those cases, respond ONLY to the person who originally posted the message. Be clear about your vote, and put it in the subject header if possible:

```
To: Tyler Spratt <tspratt@electricbagpipes.com>
Subject: YES! Cut off access! (was junk email)
From: charlie@electricbagpipes.com
───────────────────────────────────────────────────
Tyler Spratt <tspratt@electricbagpipes.com> said:
> I think that all people who waste Internet bandwidth
> should have their access cut off forever. All those who
> are in favor, send me email and I will report the count.

I am in favor of cutting off access for anyone who wastes
Internet bandwidth.
```

If you call for a vote, give detailed guidelines on *how* to vote. To save yourself some time, ask people to put their votes clearly in the subject header so that you don't have to open the message:

```
From: Tyler Spratt <tspratt@electricbagpipes.com>
Subject: access cut vote (was junk email)
To: abuse-L@electricbagpipes.com

I think that all people who waste Internet bandwidth should
have their access cut off forever.

If you are in favor of cutting off the access of people who
waste Internet bandwidth, send me (not the whole list)
email with an empty message body and the subject
     YES! cut off access
If you disagree, send me email with an empty message body
and the subject
     NO! don't cut off access
I will tally the results and post them to this list.
```

You could even use a filter to sort votes into YES and NO mailboxes.

Chain Letters

Chain letters—messages that try to convince people to redistribute it widely—are a form of computer virus. They live on computers and use naive people to spread themselves, taking up time, energy, and disk space along the way.

Be particularly cautious about messages that promise easy riches. You might be liable for criminal penalties if you advertise for a *Ponzi* or *pyramid* scheme—one where later participants send money to earlier participants. *Do not trust messages that say that the scheme is legal.* Those promises are worth as much as it cost to send the message: not much. Check with a lawyer before getting involved in anything that could possibly be a pyramid scheme.

Even well-meaning chain letters can have unpleasant results. The oldest and best example is the Craig Shergold letter. Craig was a nine-year-old boy battling cancer. He sent out a chain letter asking people to send him postcards. They did. Craig has completely recovered, and, as of this writing, is a healthy college student.

Unfortunately, thousands of postcards are still coming, causing problems for his local post office.

So while it might sound cruel to ignore the plight of some poor soul, unless you research the case enough to determine that it is legitimate *and still appropriate*, don't pass on a chain letter. Even if it is for a legitimate cause, it can get out of control.

If you *must* pass on or—yuck!—start a chain letter, at least do the following:

- Put a date, *including the year,* in the middle of the letter. If you put a date at the front or back, it is likely to get accidentally removed. If you do not put in a date, it will live on past its useful lifetime.
- Put specific information about the issue and contact information so that future recipients can easily verify it.
- Show your name and email address prominently. If you don't believe in the cause strongly enough to put your name on it, you shouldn't send it.

Hoaxes

Hoaxes are a type of chain letter that propagate urban legends. Some hoaxes are scary and some are funny. Common hoaxes include:

- warnings of new forms of criminal activity
- promotions saying a large corporation will give a large sum of money to a worthy charity if they receive a certain number of email messages
- warnings about non-existent computer viruses
- alerts about proposed governmental regulations or taxes

Hoaxes die if readers can investigate them easily. Thus, watch out for messages that don't have many concrete details. Most hoaxes don't include specific names of victims, perpetrators, or even investigating bodies. Hoaxes usually will not reference web pages or phone numbers that will give further information, nor will they give exact dates. Hoaxes usually do contain a lot of hysterical language and an urgent request to pass the message on to absolutely everybody that you know.

Armed with these guidelines, you should immediately suspect that the following is a hoax:

Subject: Re: Re: Re: DANGER!!!!

> >> I don't usually pass on chain letters, but this one is
> >> true! A friend of mine bought a Harik electric
> >> bagpipe to serenade his girlfriend with, and right
> >> after he plugged it in, it exploded! The blast was so
> >> strong that it broke his nose and her ribs! If you
> >> have a Harik bagpipe, take it in for a refund
> >> immediately, and tell everybody you know about the
> >> danger!

A message like the following is much more likely to be genuine:

Subject: bagpipe recall

Harik Bagpipes Corporation has found a problem with their
Quicksilver bagpipes. If all the drones are blocked when
the power is turned on, a feedback loop can make the bag
quite hot. After approximately 30 minutes, it can explode.

Harik Bagpipes has recalled the Quicksilver model. They
can be returned at their place of purchase or to Harik
Bagpipes directly. (Other models are not affected by this
problem.)

Our Web site has further information:
    http://www.electricbagpipes.com/prod/recall.html

I, Charlie Yzaguirre <charlie@electricbagpipes.com>, have
checked the sites mentioned. This seems to be a genuine
problem as of 20 Feb 2036. Please do not pass this on
unless you either know me personally or have checked the
Web sites. Before you pass this on, please replace my
contact information with your own.

You should investigate a story for yourself before passing it on to everyone you know. If it *is* a hoax, you might get a lot of messages pointing that out to you.

Affectionate Chain Messages

There is a type of self-replicating message that preys on love instead of fear, anger, greed, or pity. These messages have some uplifting content, followed by a command to send the message to people you feel warmly towards. They might look something like this:

```
Subject: FW: FW: Fwd: beautiful smile

>> >Your smile is beautiful!
>> >Like pentameter it whispers
>> >Delicate hurricanes of grace,
>> >Sweeter than a dream of roses.

>> >Send this message to five people who have beautiful
>> >smiles!
```

Despite the sender's good intentions, these types of sentimental messages are yet another form of virus.

Humor

Some people really like getting jokes by email. However, the practice is so common and widespread that sometimes people get overwhelmed by the number of jokes that they get. If a joke is so funny that you feel you must redistribute it, put HUMOR: in the Subject: header. That way, your correspondents can delete it quickly or save it for later.

TIP: If you pass on any original material, please attribute the author. This gives credit where credit is due and allows people to find the author if they choose.

Junk Email

You probably hate junk email. So does everybody else. Sending massive amounts of unsolicited commercial email is inconsiderate and rude.

Sending junk email probably won't get you what you want, either:

- People get so much spam now that they delete it pretty quickly. You probably won't get as many interested responses as you want.
- Your mailbox might fill with hate email and notifications of undeliverable email.
- You will lose your Internet account. Count on it.
- You might be liable for civil penalties under various anti-junk email laws.
- You might get harassed. If you give a phone number in your message, you might get thousands of people phoning to ask that you not send spam. If you have a web site, it might get attacked by anti-spam vigilantes.

Sending junk email will greatly increase the amount of email that you get—until your account gets cancelled!

Further Information on Nuisance Messages

For up-to-date information on nuisance messages, including where to find lists of current hoaxes, see

```
http://www.OvercomeEmailOverload.com/hoaxes.html
```

Educate Your Correspondents

Sometimes your friends and colleagues will send you inappropriate messages—chain letters, "me too" messages, and so on. If you are in a position of authority, you might find subordinates Cc'ing you on more than you care for. Usually, your correspondents mean well. However, if you don't let them know that you don't want such messages, they will probably do it again. That means more messages for you.

Your correspondents probably think they are doing you a favor, so you shouldn't be nasty about it. In fact, if you are not careful, you'll get an angry response back. Some templates for polite educational messages are in Chapter 6, *Spend Less Time on Responses*.

If you get a lot of messages from inside your organization, you might want to pay close attention to Chapter 11, *Improve Your Company's Email Effectiveness*. It shows how organizations can set policies and create technological aids to improve email efficiency.

Summary

To reduce the amount of email that you receive:

- Don't give out your email address. Try not to publish it anywhere on the Internet or give it to retailers. If you feel you need a public email address, get an additional email account.
- Keep track of how to communicate with the software. Remember that a piece of software performs most mailing list operations, not a human.
- Unsubscribe from some of your mailing lists. Alternatively, switch to a digest, announcements-only, or moderated list.
- Discourage responses by writing formally, explicitly mentioning that you don't need a response, and thanking in advance.
- Discourage discussions between your correspondents by making it hard for them to see and respond to each other's messages. Whenever possible, reply to the sender only instead of to everybody, use Bcc, or use named group nicknames.
- Send fewer messages. In particular, don't send junk—"me too" messages, messages that don't apply to most of the receivers, unsolicited advertisements, hoaxes, chain letters, and affectionate chain letters.
- Ask your correspondents to stop sending you inappropriate messages.

Spend Less Time on Responses

You've cut down on your incoming messages. The ones that still come through are organized and prioritized. Now you need to respond to at least some of them.

Responding to messages usually takes more time than reading messages. Composing is slower than typing: you have to think about what to say, write, rewrite, scratch your head, and rewrite again. Add in the difference between reading speed and typing speed, and you can see that writing a message takes a lot more time than reading one.

Responding to messages more efficiently can therefore save you a lot of time. This chapter will show you how to:

- **Recognize what messages don't need a response.** If you don't respond to any messages at all, you'll probably hurt your career and friendships. However, there are many cases where you don't need to respond.
- **Recognize the right time to respond.** It isn't always best to respond to a message the instant that you finish reading it.
- **Write common responses once and reuse them.** Eudora can help you to respond quickly and effortlessly to common questions.

While these techniques won't completely eliminate the time you spend on replies, they can greatly reduce it.

Don't Respond

It might make sense to ignore some messages. In a perfect world, you would have the leisure to respond to every message carefully and considerately. However, in this world, you have limited time. Furthermore, your correspondents also have limited time: they might not want you to respond.

Don't Say "Thank You" or "You're Welcome"

As mentioned in "Avoid 'Thank You' and 'You're Welcome'" on page 118, you probably don't want to regularly send messages that say only, "Thank you" and "You're welcome." It takes time for you and is probably a nuisance for your correspondents. Only send a separate thank-you message if there was an exceptional effort involved. (And if it was that exceptional, send a copy to your correspondent's boss as well.)

It is much better to give thanks in advance or the next time you have reason to send email to them.

Don't Respond to Junk Email

In almost all cases, you should not respond to junk email. While it might feel very good to fire off an angry message or to tell them to stop sending you messages, it probably won't do you much good. A lot of junk email comes from temporary or non-existent accounts, so your message might come right back to you.

Responding might even *increase* the amount of junk email you get. By giving any reply at all, you let the senders know that your address has a real, live person attached to it. That makes your address more valuable to junk emailers.

If you want to take effective action to people who send junk email, you'll need a fair amount of technical sophistication and time. The excellent book *Stopping Spam* by Alan Schwarz and Simson Garfinkel (O'Reilly & Associates, 1998) explains the procedure in detail. However, if you had enough free time to take effective action, you probably wouldn't be reading my book.

Don't Answer Messages from Strangers

You do not need to respond to email from strangers. While this might sound mean, the time you spend on strangers is time you aren't spending on the people who matter to you.

If you have any sort of public persona, you might end up getting so many messages from strangers that it can take a long time to answer them all. Thirty minutes, an hour, four hours—at some point you have to stop. While it would be nice of you to respond, it isn't reasonable for people to expect that you will always do so.

TIP: If you send email to a stranger, be pleasant and acknowledge that he or she is doing you a favor. Say "please" and "thank you" prominently.

Don't Respond to Mailing List Loops

It is a good idea to not respond to any sort of multi-person email arguments. Occasionally, people will get caught in a nasty, self-perpetuating loop between people trying to help and people that they annoy by helping. I saw this happen once:

- Someone subscribed a large number of people to a mailing list without their knowledge or permission. Furthermore, the list was misconfigured so that the list server address and the list name address were the same.
- A lot of people tried to unsubscribe.
- Many people wrote to the list saying something along the lines of, "Look, you idiots, don't write to the list to unsubscribe! Unsubscribe like this …"
- A bunch of people wrote to the list saying, "I'm not an idiot, the list is misconfigured!"
- More people wrote to the list saying, "Please don't send any more messages about unsubscribing!"
- Even more people wrote to the list saying, "Please don't send any more messages telling people not to explain how to unsubscribe!"
- People responded by saying, "Come on, don't be so mean! I made a simple mistake—you don't have to jump all over me!"

Hundreds of messages went back and forth until unsubscribing was fixed.

The more people on a list, the more likely that such an argument will start; the more people on a list, the more likely that such an argument will get out of control.

If you see a list getting locked into a bad loop like this, shut up and stay out of it. Giving advice almost always makes it worse, unfortunately.

Look at How You Were Addressed

You can sometimes tell if you need to respond to a message by looking at the location of your email address in the message headers. In general, you don't usually need to respond unless:

1. you are in the To: header, *and*
2. the message is from someone you have responsibilities towards, *and*
3. the sender has a question.

If you are in the Cc: header, then you probably should *not* respond unless there is something wrong in the message. Most people don't want to get messages like this:

```
From: betsy@flossrecycling.com
To: liz@flossrecycling.com
Cc: john@flossrecycling.com, jim@flossrecycling.com,
    donald@flossrecycling.com, charles@flossrecycling.com,
    maryjane@flossrecycling.com
Subject: Re: Release 3.1.4.2

I got your message about the change orders.
```

The one exception: you *should* respond, even if you are only on the Cc: list, if something in the message is incorrect or a problem. For example, suppose a message gave arrangements for a meeting for next Tuesday. If you know that the entire division will be at a conference next Tuesday, you should alert the sender.

Figuring out how you should respond when you are in the Bcc: header is a little trickier. Because Bcc: is sometimes used to spare people from follow-up discussions, it isn't always obvious if you should act as if you were in the To: header or the Cc: header. You probably want to act as if you were in the Cc: header unless there is an obvious request to you in the body of the message.

Be careful with the rule about direct questions: sometimes the sender will have a question but not ask it explicitly. For example the sender might discuss an issue but never actually say that they want a response:

```
Subject: report covers

Jeff -

I was thinking about the report covers. Blue might be
better than teal.

--
Mabel
```

In this case, Mabel didn't actually ask, "What do you think?" but the question is implied. Treat this as a direct question and give a response.

If you need to respond to a message, but won't be able to answer for a few days, it is polite to send a message back. Don't just say that you got the message, however. Say what you need to complete the action and when you expect that the action will be completed:

```
To: Charlie Yzaguirre <charlie@electricbagpipes.com>
From: Jessica Robinson <jessica@electricbagpipes.com>
Subject: Re: Friday card game

Charlie -

I don't know if I will be able to join you to play cards. My
trial starts on Monday, and I might be busy for five to ten
years after that.

I will phone you by Friday morning if I will be able to
join you for cards.
```

Read All Messages on a Topic before Responding to Any

Frequently, you are better off reading all of the messages on a topic before responding to any of them. This will help you avoid time-wasting sequences like this:

- Jamshid reads a question on a mailing list.
- Jamshid answers the question.
- Mabel reads the question.
- Mabel answers the question.
- Mabel reads Jamshid's answer.
- Mabel feels stupid.
- Everyone else on the list gets annoyed at having to read two answers to the question.

Here's another common sequence:

- Jose emails a question to Mabel.
- Jose finds the answer on his own.
- Jose sends a message telling Mabel not to bother with the question.
- Mabel reads Jose question.
- Mabel spends an hour researching the question.
- Mabel sends Jose an answer.
- Mabel reads that Jose didn't need the answer.
- Mabel feels stupid.

Don't be like Mabel! If you read all the messages on the same topic before replying to any, then you will know if someone else answered any questions raised. This will save you from composing unneeded messages. As discussed in the introduction to Chapter 2, using filters to group related messages makes it much easier to see if there are further messages on a topic.

You might worry that if you don't respond immediately, you will forget to reply. The best way to remember to reply is to create a response window (with the question quoted) as soon as you see that you might need to respond. Then, read all the other messages. If someone else answers the question, you can close the response window. If nobody addressed the issue, the response window will still be open when you finish reading your messages, reminding you to respond.

If you get a message that has multiple issues, it's best to create one response window for each issue, editing each so it has a quote for only that issue. That way, you can keep track of each issue independently.

Use Prewritten Responses

If you send a few basic messages over and over again, consider saving those responses somewhere so that you don't have to retype them. Eudora will let you store prewritten responses or *stationery* that you can use to respond quickly.

To create stationery with Eudora for Mac OS:

- Open the Stationery Window by selecting Window→Stationery.
- Click on the New button in the lower left corner.
- Give the new stationery a name.
- Click on the Edit button. A message composition window will appear.
- Type in your message.
- Click on the Save button in the upper right-hand corner of the message composition window.

To create stationery with Eudora for Windows:

- Open the Stationery Window by selecting Tools→Stationery.
- Right-click in the window.
- Select New. A message composition window will appear.
- Type in your message.
- Select File→Save As Stationery.
- Type in the name of the stationery,
- Click on the Save button.

Be sure to be *extremely* polite in your prewritten responses. If all goes well, you'll be using these form letters over and over again, including times when you are tired and/or the person sending the message is in a bad mood. If you are not careful now, someday you'll get an angry response to your stationery messages.

If your prewritten message is vague, you can use it more often than if it is specific. The disadvantage, of course, is that vague responses are more likely to be ambiguous. (I cover ambiguity in great detail in Chapter 7, *Reduce Ambiguity*.) Sorry. Life is full of difficult choices.

To use stationery, select `Message`→`Reply With…` and select the stationery that you want to use. You can also quickly add text from stationery to a message by dragging the stationery from the `Stationery Window` to the message composition window.

The rest of this section covers examples of some prewritten responses.

Give Directions

Writing good directions takes a lot of time. It is a good idea to write and save good, clear directions for each route:

```
To get to Floss Recycling's headquarters from Highway 914:
+ Take the Tubman exit north (towards downtown).
+ Take Tubman Road through three stop lights and turn left
  at the Lion's Pride restaurant. That's Goa Way, but the
  sign is hard to see.
+ Take Goa Way for six blocks. Floss Recycling Inc. is on
  the right-hand side in the big building painted like a
  floss dispenser.
----
To get to Floss Recycling's headquarters from the airport:
+ Follow Erhart Road out of the airport until you come to a
  fork in the road; take the right fork. You will then be on
  Goa Way.
+ Take Goa Way for six blocks. Floss Recycling Inc. is on
  the left-hand side in the big building painted like a
  floss dispenser.
```

If you know that someone is coming from a particular direction, you can quickly edit out all the directions that you don't need:

```
Subject: Re: site visit

Jamaal --

I'm happy that we will finally meet. I think you will find
that Floss Recycling Inc. is a fun place to work.

To get to Floss Recycling's headquarters from the airport:
+ Follow Erhart Road out of the airport until you come to a
  fork in the road; take the right fork. You will then be on
  Goa Way.
+ Take Goa Way for six blocks. Floss Recycling Inc. is on
  the left-hand side in the big building painted like a
  floss dispenser.
```

Respond to Vague Questions

Some people write email that is difficult to figure out. (They haven't read Chapter 7, *Reduce Ambiguity*, yet.) Frequently the question will be too vague, like:

```
Subject: campus information

Please send me information about the University of
East-Central Illinois at Hoopston.
```

This gives no clue about what the sender wants: admission application deadlines? The number of faculty? The acreage? The number of buildings? The name of the Engineering Dean's dog?

If you are in a position where you get vague questions regularly, you can save time by developing an all-purpose response that suggests places to go for further information. For example:

```
I'm sorry, but your message wasn't specific enough for me
to determine what interested you about the University of
East-Central Illinois at Hoopston.

If you were interested in admissions, see
    http://www.admit.ueci-h.edu/

If you were interested in research, see
    http://www.ueci-h.edu/academics.html

If you were interested in sports, see
    http://www.sports.ueci-h.edu/GoBrooms.htm

If you were interested in alumni activities, see
    http://www.alumni.ueci-h.edu/alumni.htm

You can also try searching the University of East-Central
Illinois at Hoopston web from
    http://www.ueci-h.edu/searchpage.html

Good luck in your search.
```

Hopefully, this will either answer the question or make the questioner understand that he or she will have better luck if they ask their questions more carefully.

TIP: If you want people who send you vague questions to leave you alone, make your all-purpose answer very long, boring, and impersonal. It will make them think that you are busy and uninteresting.

Even if you can't write a response like the previous example, you can still create a stationery message for responding to vague messages. You might want stationery like this:

```
I'm sorry, I couldn't figure out what you wanted. Please
tell me
        + What *exact* area of the subject interests you?
          Please be specific.
        + What level of detail do you need?
        + What level of expertise do you have in this area?
        + What have you tried already?

Frequently, if you tell me what you will do with the
information, that will answer several of the questions at
once.
```

"I'm Busy"

You can also use stationery to tell people that you can't give them much attention. For example:

```
I'm furiously getting ready for the Floss Recycling Expo,
so don't have much time for email. I read your message, but
unfortunately don't have time to respond thoughtfully. I'll
get back to you soon after Floss Recycling Expo finishes on
28 Jan.
```

Responses to Mass Mailings

As mentioned in "Educate Your Correspondents" on page 133, you might need to ask people to not send you mass mailings. A carefully written stationery message that asks people not to send you mass mailings can save you a lot of time. This section has examples of stationery you might want to use for discouraging nuisance email.

Hoax Responses

Hoaxes can be extremely annoying, as mentioned in Chapter 5, *Reduce the Number of Incoming Messages*. If you get hoaxes regularly, you can use stationery like the following:

```
I applaud your public spirit in wanting to help all of us
out, but this message has all the trappings of a hoax:
+ It uses lots of emotionally charged language.
+ It gives few specifics.
+ It is essentially impossible to verify: it does not give
    contact information for the original author, names of
    victims, perpetrators, or investigating bodies.  There
    is no URL for further information.
+ It has no date.
+ It implores the readers to pass it on to everybody they
    know.

Hoaxes are a form of computer virus: they use unsuspecting
readers to replicate and transmit the hoax. For more
information on hoaxes, see
http://istpub.berkeley.edu:4201/bcc/Nov_Dec98/gen.hoax.html
http://www.symantec.com/avcenter/hoax.html

I know that you wanted to help, but I get approximately 80
messages per day. Please do not send me any other
mass-mailings in the future unless you check them out
carefully yourself.
```

Chain Letters

For chain letters, you could try sending a message similar to the hoax message in the previous section, or you could just explain why you don't want to participate:

> I appreciate that you thought of me, but I'm not interested in any sort of chain letters. Many chain letters are hoaxes or illegal. Even those that are valid when they are created frequently spin out of control -- especially if they don't have a date mentioned somewhere.
>
> I am thus unwilling to pass on a chain letter unless I can check it out very carefully myself. And, given that I already get about 80 email messages per day, I don't have time to investigate them.
>
> I know you thought I'd like to read the message, but please do me a favor and don't send me any more chain letters.
>
> Thanks!
>
> P.S. For more on chain letters, see
>   http://chainletters.org

Humor Glut Responses

If you like getting jokes, but find them distracting, here is useful stationery to send:

I appreciate you thinking of me and like the jokes you send, but I get approximately 80 pieces of email per day, making it tough for me to see what is urgent and what is not. While the jokes are nice, they make it even harder to see what is important.

If you could put 'HUMOR:' at the beginning of a subject line, then I could set up my email program to automatically put jokes in another mailbox. That way I could still read the jokes, but at some time when I am not so busy.

Could you do that for me? I know that's asking extra work from you; if that's too much to ask, then (*sigh*) would you mind taking me off of your jokes mailing list?

Again, I appreciate your jokes but just don't have the time to deal with them in my inbox.

Thanks in advance!

You can then set up your filters to quietly put messages with HUMOR in the subject header into a jokes mailbox, as shown in "File Jokes" on page 70.

Ask for Bcc:

As mentioned in "Use Bcc: Instead of To: or Cc:" on page 123, you'll get fewer messages if you are in the Bcc: header instead of the To: header. If you get a lot of messages that have a huge list of people in the To: header, you might want stationery like this:

> Could you do me a favor, please?
>
> In the future, when you send out a large mailing like the one I just got from you, could you please put the addresses on the BCC line instead of on the TO or CC line?
>
> When all the addresses are on the TO or CC line:
>
> 1) Everyone can see all the addresses. Some people prefer to keep their addresses private.
> 2) Some people (depending upon their email software) have to wade through all the addresses to get to the body of the message.
> 3) If someone does a REPLY-TO-ALL by accident (instead of a simple REPLY to just you), everybody on the address list will get that message - which might not be relevant to anyone but you.
>
> BCC keeps the addresses private, so none of those problems can occur.
>
> I know you weren't deliberately trying to cause problems, and hope you aren't offended by this message. I just wanted to let you know of a better way.
>
> Thanks!

Use Auto-Responders

If you are using Paid or Sponsored mode, you can set up your filters to respond automatically to messages. This is useful but dangerous: you might respond inappropriately if your filters misfire. For example, suppose that Rose Winkle, the chief operations officer, sends Mabel a message on the Payroll Department's budget. If Mabel's filters send a message about rose gardening in response to messages that have `rose` in the header, Rose Winkle will be pretty surprised!

However, if you are absolutely overwhelmed by messages, you could respond with a generic form that gives some information and tells how to bypass the automatic response and get to you. One way to give people a way past your automatic response is to tell people a secret word that bypasses your filters.

Put the secret word on a separate line to make it more obvious.

```
Hi --

I get a lot of email, much of it unsolicited commercial
messages. I thus ignore any message that comes from an
address that I don't recognize.

If you are looking for information on roses, please see
    http://www.rosegardens.org

If you are looking for information on the Hoopston
Hollering Hangar Honchos, please see
    http://www.hangarhonchos.org

If you are a real human being and that didn't answer your
question, send your message again but put the word
    KERSHNUGLE
in the subject line. I'll see the word and read your
message.

Sorry to inconvenience you.
```

To respond to messages from strangers that don't have the secret word in the subject, you need to change the default (last) filter in your filter list. (See "Default Filter: I Don't Know You" on page 85):

<table>
<tr><td>
when the message comes in or manual filtering is selected
if Subject: contains KERSHNUGLE,
then Skip Rest
</td></tr>
<tr><td>
when the message comes in or manual filtering is selected
if «Any Header» contains .,
then Reply With→stationery that you choose,
    Transfer To→z-UnrecognizedAddress, and
    Skip Rest
</td></tr>
</table>

You should put these filters *after* ones for getting rid of junk email. Otherwise, you will respond to junk emailers automatically.

Notify That You're Out of the Office

One of the most common uses of auto-responders is to let senders know that the receiver will not be able to read a message for a while:

```
I will be at Floss Expo from Monday, January 18 to Friday,
January 27. I don't know how often I will be able to check
my email until I return.

If you have urgent questions about the Payroll Department,
please contact Chantelle Williams at x2202.
```

Unfortunately, because of how email is delivered, setting up an out-of-office message isn't always easy to do. You could set up a filter to always respond, but the filter will only be activated if Eudora is running. If you turn off your computer before you go (or if it crashes right away), nobody will get your out-of-office message.

Where does your email go when your computer is off? It stays on the *email server*—a computer that is on all the time and whose job it is to receive and hold your mail. Thus the "right" way to set up an out-of-office message is to tell the email server to give an out-of-office message.

There are many different email server programs, and each has its own way of doing out-of-office messages. Worse, you might not have access to the email server. The best thing to do is to go to your Information Technology group and say, "I want to set up an out-of-office message on my email account. What do I need to do?" (You might also suggest that they set up a Web-based interface for managing out-of-office messages; see "Out-of-Office Messages" on page 223.)

TIP: If you set up an out-of-office message, don't forget to turn it off when you get back.

Dangers of Auto-Responders

Auto-responders can be very handy, but you need to be careful. Your auto-responder can get caught in a loop. Take the following situation:

- Mabel goes on vacation.
- Andy sends Mabel email.
- Andy goes on vacation.
- Mabel's email program sends Andy a message that Mabel's out of the office.
- Andy's email program sends Mabel a message that Andy is out of the office.
- Mabel's email program sends Andy a message that Mabel's out of the office.
- Andy's email program sends Mabel a message that Andy's out of the office.
- repeat until Andy or Mabel get back from vacation...

Any sort of automatic response can get into a loop, but out-of-office messages are particularly likely to get caught in this kind of loop. During a vacation in January 2000, a major U.S. university had so many "I'm out of the office" loops that they had to take the entire email system down.

You should thus be very careful about autoresponses, especially out-of-office messages. Here are some steps to take to avoid loops:

- Do not reply automatically to messages from your hobby or announcement mailing lists. (You might want to temporarily unsubscribe to your mailing lists until you are back.)
- Do not reply automatically to *bounce* messages—automatic responses that tell you that a message that you sent couldn't be delivered.
- If possible, only send one message per week to any address. If someone sends you a lot of messages on a regular basis, he or she could get bored with your auto-response.

You should probably ask your system administrator for help setting up your automatic responses.

Summary

- Recognize that you don't have to answer or even read every single message.
- Attach your thanks to other messages. Don't send a thank-you in its own message unless the effort was exceptional.
- You do not need to respond to strangers.
- If you ask questions of strangers, be sure to be very polite. Say "please" and thank them in advance.
- A long and boring all-purpose response will discourage further correspondence.
- If you are in the Cc: header, you shouldn't respond unless there is something incorrect in the message.
- Read all messages on a topic before responding to any of them, but open a response window immediately if you think you might need to reply.
- Use prewritten responses.
- If you use an automatic response system, give a magic word so that people can get your attention if the prewritten response doesn't answer their question.
- Don't respond automatically to mailing lists.
- Don't forget to turn off out-of-office messages when you return.

CHAPTER 7

Reduce Ambiguity

Ambiguous messages waste time. At best, your correspondents will need to ask for further information. This will add to the stack of messages you have to deal with: at least one more message to write, at least one more message to read.

Worse, your correspondents might ignore the message. You'll have to send more email to get them to act.

At worst, your correspondents won't realize that they didn't understand your message and will do the *wrong* thing. You'll have to spend more time (and email messages) trying to correct the situation.

You might find that you have more trouble making your meaning clear in email than you do in other communications media. This is not surprising: you probably got lots of training on how to write paper documents, some on how to speak, and none on how to write email.

Training on how to write paper documents won't, by itself, teach how to write email well. Centuries of improvements in printing technologies have led to variations in paper and typography styles. These differences can give clues to the content of the document: the Bickham Script font *(Bickham Script)* is for formal invitations while Greymantle (Greymantle) is for stories of elves and fairies. Email, by contrast, is so new that it doesn't have enough variation to give the same type of clues. Furthermore, because email messages move so quickly and are so easy to reply to, they tend to be dialogues like speech, not monologues like paper correspondence.

Email has some similarities to spoken communication, but isn't exactly like speech. The printed word doesn't convey gestures, intonation, or facial expression. This means that knowing how to speak well also doesn't automatically mean knowing how to write email well, either.

This chapter examines in further detail how email is different and how to properly convey your meaning.

Provide Adequate Context

Without adequate *context*—information about a message's environment or situation—messages are not as understandable. Consider the following newspaper headline:

```
Bulls and Bears Face Similar Challenges
```

If you are from North America, this headline will have at least three different meanings. If it is in the business section, the headline is about stockmarket analysts or investors. If the headline is in the sports section, it refers to professional sports teams based in Chicago. In the science section, the headline is about large mammals. The headline is perfectly understandable with adequate context and ambiguous without it.

Unfortunately, email messages don't provide much context. By and large, email messages all look the same regardless of who sent them, where in the world they came from, and what they are about. A message could be a budget forecast, party invitation, joke, or request for information. Adequate context is essential.

Quote the Previous Messages

As you probably have already seen, a simple and effective way for you to give context to a very brief response is to quote from the previous message. You've probably been annoyed by colleagues who send messages like this:

```
Subject: Re: progress

no
```

When your correspondents quote some of the previous message, they are much more understandable:

```
Subject: Re: progress

>Are you going to have the budget estimates done by
>Thursday?

no
```

Make References Concrete

A common problem with lack of context comes from words that take the place of things that aren't mentioned in the message:

```
Subject: Re: cover selection

I talked to them about it, and they want to see the other
one before they make up their minds.
```

Even if the writer quotes some of the previous message, the reader might still have to struggle to figure out what *them*, *it*, *they*, and *the other one* refer to.

While you need to avoid references to missing things in any kind of writing, it is a particular problem in email because it feels so much like a conversation. If you are responding to a message that you just received, it might feel like you don't need to explain what you're talking about. However, unlike a face-to-face conversation, you won't notice when your correspondent shifts his or her attention to other things. Your correspondent might have six hours of meetings between sending a message and reading your response.

Fortunately, you have a good chance of spotting potential problems by looking for certain types of words. Carefully examine your message for the following place-holding words and consider using more specific words:

- pronouns (such as *his, it,* or *those*)
- common names (such as *Chris* or *Dave*)
- concept holders (such as *information* or *data*)
- relative expressions of place (such as *here* or *there*)
- relative expressions of time (such as *today* or *next Wednesday*)

Pronouns

Using pronouns for people or things that aren't explicitly mentioned is a very common problem:

```
Subject: Re: rose garden tour

He said that he would give me a tour if you would lend him
the keys. Could you get the keys to him by Saturday?
```

Examine any pronouns carefully, particularly in your first three sentences, and replace any that are ambiguous:

```
Subject: Re: rose garden tour

Ezra said that he would give me a tour if you would lend
him the keys. Could you get the keys to Ezra by Saturday?
```

Common Names

Common names can be almost as confusing as pronouns. *Chris* might be *Christine Olszewski, Christopher Chien*, or *Christiaan Phrockmeijer*. (A friend worked at a place where ten percent of the employees were named *Mike*. There were a few groups that even had two people with the same first *and* last name.) Minor variations in spelling can also confuse people: which coworker is *Ann* and which is *Anne*?

If you mention someone whose name is common, do at least one of the following:

- write out enough of the name to make it unambiguous
- give their email ID (like *jsmith* or *rowilliams*)
- mention the person's position in the organization

Concepts

Placeholders for concepts, like *idea*, *data*, and *information* are warning signs that your message might be too vague. Questions like this are difficult to answer:

```
Subject: information

Please send me information.
```

Your correspondents will reply faster, more accurately, and more completely if you get rid of words that refer to concepts:

```
Subject: UECI-H history

Are there any Web pages about the history of practical
jokes at the University of East Central Illinois' Hoopston
campus?
```

Places

Here is a very imprecise word in cyberspace. Given that people can access their email from just about anywhere, *here* could be a workplace, a home, a hotel, or even an Internet cafe. *There* is even more ambiguous, since it refers to where you *think* that the receiver will read the message, not where the receiver *does* read the message. Be very specific when you refer to places.

Time

Times and dates can also lose their meaning. Words like *yesterday, today, tomorrow, last Monday,* and *next month* are dangerous in email. *Next Thursday* might pass before your correspondents—or whomever they forward the message to—see the message. Although your messages contain the date and time that you sent them, that information might get lost when the message is forwarded. Thus, you should always spell out dates fully. Times should include not just AM or PM, but also the time zone if there is any possibility of misunderstanding.

Typographical errors in dates are very easy to make, and can have disastrous consequences. It is a good idea to mention the day of the week. Then, if the day of the week doesn't match the date, your correspondent has a chance to notice that something is wrong.

Examples: Bad and Good

Here is an example of a message with ambiguities in place, time, and concept:

```
Subject: meeting

Hi - Can you come here for an informational meeting next
Monday at 8?
```

People will be more likely to come to the right place at the right time for the right reasons if the message reads as follows:

```
Subject: RGC meeting Mon 1/19?

Hi - Can you come to a meeting of the Rose Gardening Club
next Tuesday, 19 Jan 2038 at 8 PM? Ezra P. Snodwhistle will
give a report on last month's meeting (5 Dec 2037) with the
Pest Control Superintendent. The meeting will be in the
Waldo Room of the Hoopston Third National Bank.
```

Putting information in a table can help the information stand out:

```
Subject: RGC meeting Mon 1/19?

Hi - Can you come to a meeting of the Rose Gardening Club?
Ezra P. Snodwhistle will give a report on last month's
meeting (5 Dec 2037) with the Pest Control Superintendent.

DATE: Tuesday, 19 Jan 2038
TIME: 8 PM
PLACE: The Waldo Room of the Hoopston Third National Bank
```

Repeat Subject in the Body

Providing the appropriate context does no good if people don't notice it. In particular, people frequently don't pay close attention to the Subject: header. I once saw someone send a message like this to a large group of people:

```
Subject: Mama Del's 2/6 ... party 530-730p

Please join us in celebrating Mabel's 45th birthday at Mama
Del's! Appetizers at 5:30 PM, pizza at 6:00 PM.
```

About a fifth of the people didn't notice the 2/6 in the subject header and wrote to ask the date of the party. The moral of the story: always repeat any important header information in the body of the message.

Ask Detailed Questions

You need to be particularly careful about context in messages that are not responses to a previous message. Your correspondent can't look up the previous message, so you need to be very clear.

Questions are most likely to need more context. If there is something you don't know about or don't understand, you're more likely to be vague—which could frustrate your correspondent. You'd probably be frustrated, too, if you got messages like this:

```
Subject: heating system
```

```
Please tell me about the building heating system.
```

Is this a question about the layout of the heating ducts? What type of wiring the system uses? What brand of controllers the system uses?

If you are going to ask a question—particularly of someone you haven't met before—you need to frame your question carefully. If your question is too broad or vague, your correspondent might ignore it, delay responding, or send it back to you with a request for more details. Be sure to answer the following questions:

- Which specific aspect of the subject interests you?
- How much detail do you need?
- How knowledgeable are you already in the subject?

Frequently, if you explain what you plan to do with the information, that will answer the first two questions implicitly. For example:

```
Subject: building heating system
```

```
Christopher,

The conference rooms on the seventh floor are either too
hot or too cold. I'd like to reset the temperatures in all
three conference rooms.

Please tell me about the building heating system.
```

The second message is better than the first, but it would be even better with detailed questions:

```
Subject: building heating system

Christopher,

The conference rooms on the seventh floor are either too
hot or too cold. I'd like to reset the temperatures in all
three conference rooms.

+ Can I reset the thermostats, or is that something that
Facilities has to do?

+ If I can reset the thermostats, how do I do so? I looked
at what I believe were the thermostats, and I couldn't find
any knobs or dials on them.

Thanks!
```

Say What Action You Want

You can also be unclear if you don't explicitly say what you want to happen. In spoken conversations, the context usually makes it clear if you are expressing a desire, an opinion, a fact, an order, or a question. In email, it is not as clear. For example, look at the following message:

```
From: Mabel Garcia <mabel@flossrecycling.com>
To: Jeff Chee <jeffc@flossrecycling.com>
Subject: report covers

I was thinking about the report covers. Blue might be
better than yellow.
```

Why did Mabel send Jeff a message about the report cover colors?

- Is Mabel ordering Jeff to change the color of the report cover?
- Is Mabel expressing an opinion that Jeff can ignore if he chooses?
- Does Mabel know a fact about the covers that makes blue a better choice than yellow?
- Does Mabel want Jeff's opinion on the color?
- Does Mabel want to know if there is a penalty for changing the cover color?

Mabel's message would be clearer if she were more explicit:

```
Subject: report covers

I was thinking about the report covers. Blue might be
better than yellow.

Would there be any problem with changing the cover color?
+ Is blue more expensive?
+ Would blue clash with the other artwork?
+ Would changing the color delay production?

Please find out the answers to these questions and get back
to me.
```

"Vocal" Techniques for Reducing Ambiguity

Email shares many traits with verbal conversations; people give fast, short contributions that they can't take back. Because of the similarity, people tend to write exactly what they would say out loud. However, without the emphasis and pauses of spoken language, it is easy for your correspondents to interpret something differently than how you intended. This section will show how to use text to simulate vocal expressions.

Use "Intonational" Grouping

Pauses in speech help to group together sets of words. The following might be perfectly understandable in speech, but is unclear in text:

```
Subject: summer picnic menu
────────────────────────────────────────────────

It's time for the annual summer picnic!  Which menu option
would you like: hot dogs with lime gelatin, or lasagna with
corn on the cob or green bean casserole?
```

Is the green bean casserole a main dish or a side dish that goes with lasagna?

While a standard use of commas can make such groupings unambiguous, the sender and the receiver have to both agree on what "standard use" is. In American English, a comma is optional after the next-to-last item in a list. Furthermore, poor understanding of comma rules is common.

It is much safer to use spaces, tabs, and carriage returns to make the grouping clear:

```
Subject: summer picnic menu
────────────────────────────────────────────────

It's time for the annual summer picnic!

Which menu option would you like:
+ hot dogs with lime gelatin
+ lasagna with
    corn on the cob or
    green bean casserole?
```

Some people like to make numbered outlines:

```
Subject: summer picnic menu

It's time for the annual summer picnic!

Which menu option would you like:
1. hot dogs with lime gelatin
2. lasagna with
      2a. corn on the cob or
      2b. green bean casserole?
```

Numbered outlines do make things very clear, but they can encourage people to respond with just a number. If you send messages with numbered lists, be prepared for responses that look like this:

```
Subject: Re: summer picnic menu

2b
```

Repeating *all* the information takes more work, but is the clearest of all:

```
Subject: summer picnic menu

It's time for the annual summer picnic!

Which menu option would you like:
      + hot dogs with lime gelatin
      + lasagna with corn on the cob
      + lasagna with green bean casserole?
```

An **advantage** of this last style is that it becomes very easy to quote the important part of the message. You're likely to get more concise and understandable responses:

```
Subject: Re: summer picnic menu

I would like:
    >+ lasagna with corn on the cob
```

Use Emphasis

In speech, emphasis helps eliminate ambiguity. For example, the following sentence is unclear without emphasis:

> I said that I would go to the store tomorrow.

Am I conveying the message that I am hurt that you doubted my promise?

> I *said* that I would go to the store tomorrow.

Am I clarifying that I'm not going to the garden?

> I said that I would go to the *store* tomorrow.

Am I telling when I plan on going to the store?

> I said that I would go to the store *tomorrow.*

It is true that I could rewrite the message to eliminate the ambiguity:

> As I explained already, I can't go to the store today. I will go tomorrow.

However, it is easy to overlook that an ambiguity exists. It *is* generally obvious where you should put emphasis. You should add emphasis even if you don't think something is ambiguous.

While Eudora lets you put words into italics, your correspondent's email program might not be able to display them. (Chapter 9, *Make Messages Legible*, explores the issue of differing presentation capabilities.) If you don't know what your correspondent's email program can display, it is far safer to use plain text. Instead of italics, you can show emphasis with asterisks. Thus the previous example could be written in email as:

```
Subject: shopping trip

I said that I would go to the store *tomorrow*.
```

Summary

Ambiguous messages waste time. Your correspondents will be more likely to understand and respond to your messages properly if you:

- Quote the previous message.
- Rewrite your message to eliminate placeholders for people, places, dates, times, and concepts.
- Use whitespace—carriage returns, tabs, and spaces—to show how words should be grouped together.
- Emphasize words that you would stress in conversation.
- Ask for the result that you want.
- Frame questions carefully. Explain what specific aspect of the subject you are interested in, what level of detail you need, and what level of expertise you have.

Convey Emotional Tone

You have probably already seen how destructive a *flame war*—a series of angry email messages—can be. An organization can take hours to clean up after even a minor battle. Besides generating an enormous number of messages, flame wars are emotionally draining. Reducing your participation in flame wars is a very good way to improve your email productivity.

Why is it so much easier to make someone mad with an email message than in a face-to-face conversation? Because text lacks not only vocal inflection but also body language. There is no twinkling of the eyes to say you are kidding, no slapping the back of your hand to show urgency or frustration, no slouching or slumping to display discouragement. Unfortunately, without these cues, it is easy for your correspondents to misinterpret your underlying emotion.

In addition, you can't see your correspondents' mood. In a face-to-face talk, if you see that someone is having a really bad day, you will adjust your message appropriately. You won't tell a joke to someone who you can see is grieving.

Finally, email doesn't have a built-in "cooling off" period. The combatants can send responses immediately—they don't have to wait until they see the other person or until the postal carrier comes to pick up a letter. Email arguments thus can escalate very rapidly.

Paid and Sponsored versions of Eudora 5 have a feature called "Mood Watch" which is designed to let you know when a message is offensive, but there are a lot of messages that might be offensive that it won't catch. While you should definitely pay attention if Eudora marks an outgoing message with chili peppers, don't feel safe Eudora doesn't mark it.

Even if you don't make someone angry, not conveying your emotional tone well can lead to significant misunderstandings. It is important to be able to express urgency and uncertainty in messages.

Fortunately, there are a number of conventions that you can use to help express your emotional tone. These include representations of body language and vocal inflection, as well as markers for urgency and uncertainty. This chapter discusses these techniques.

Use Stand-ins for Gestures and Facial Expression

You've probably already seen *emoticons*—textual pictures of faces—in electronic mail messages. By far, the most common three are

> :-) *smiley*, which means, "I'm happy"
>
> ;-) *winky*, which means, "I'm kidding"
>
> :-(*frowny*, which means, "I'm sad or disappointed"

While there are numerous others from ill (%^P) to angry (>:-<) to astonished (:-o), these are much less common and so more open to misinterpretation.

TIP: People also sometimes use <grin> or <g> to show a smile.

TIP: Recognize that emoticons won't have much meaning to people whose email goes through a text-to-speech processor: imagine a computer reading a "winky" emoticon: "semi-colon dash close parenthesis..." Some text-to-speech processors leave out punctuation completely! If you think your correspondent might be using a text-to-speech processor, take the extra time to be explicit about your emotions.

Some people say that emoticons should never ever be used in business communications. I feel that it depends upon what type of communication it is. If you are wisecracking to your good friend in the office across from you, it is probably appropriate. If it is the vice-president addressing everyone in the division, it is likely to be less appropriate. If it is a message to the CEO of your favorite foreign client, it is probably not a good idea:

```
Subject: negotiations

Dear Watanabe-san:

I look forward to our meeting on Tuesday, 19 February,
2038.

I feel confident that we can find solutions to all the
outstanding issues concerning the merger of our two
enterprises. :-)


--
Patricia Nguyen
President and CEO, Floss Recycling Incorporated
```

Think of it this way: if it is a solemn enough message that it would be impolite to laugh if you said it in person, you shouldn't use a smiley face in email. If you might laugh in person, it's reasonable to convey that in email.

Express Uncertainty

Paper documents are usually designed to be *persuasive*. Authors usually avoid expressing any doubt so the audience will take their side of an issue. Email messages, on the other hand, are usually *collaborative*: people normally use email to find a consensus. This difference in purpose means that it is much more important to express your certainty level in email than in paper documents.

For example, suppose that the vice-president asked you how long it will take to finish a project. If you sound too certain, the vice-president might commit the entire division to an unreasonably early goal. Such a misunderstanding can lead to flame wars or damage your career.

Unless you are very certain what people will do with information that you give them, you should try to show when you have doubts about your information.

Punctuation

Here are some typographical tricks you can use to show uncertainty.

You've probably already seen (?) to indicate uncertainty or (sp?) when someone isn't sure about the spelling of a word:

```
Subject: Re: CTO

>What's the name of the Chief Financial Officer?

Chris Olshefsky(sp?). She's been CFO for two (?) years.
```

I like to use a leading and trailing question mark when there is an entire phrase that is uncertain:

```
Subject: lunch meeting

I just had lunch with Chris Olszewski, who is the ?first
female CFO? of Floss Recycling Technologies, Inc.
```

In this case, I want to show that I think there were no chief financial officers who were female before Chris got the job. Putting (?) after "first", "female", or "chief financial officer" could be misinterpreted. For example, if I put a question mark after "female", the reader might think that I wasn't sure if Chris was female or not!

Several dots can symbolize a pause. This can be an indication that the sender is either discouraged or uncertain:

```
Subject: Re: CFO

>What's the name of the Chief Financial Officer?

Her name... oh yeah, Chris Olszewski. I wish I were moving
up as fast in the world as she is...
```

Short Utterances

While most people think that "um" and "uh" are mistakes to be avoided at all costs, they actually have a purpose in verbal conversations. In a conversation, listeners get uncomfortable if there is too much silence in a sentence. They don't know if the speaker is still composing his or her thoughts or if he or she has gone mentally missing. "Uh" and "um" alert the listener that the speaker is having trouble formulating speech, and it will take a moment for the sentence to resume.

Similarly, you can use "um" and uh" in your email to show that you're having difficulty answering the question:

> Subject: Re: brochures supply
>
> >How many boxes of brochures do we have left?
>
> Um. Seventeen, as I recall.

Clearly, you could write out that you are unsure:

> Subject: Re: brochure supply
>
> >How many boxes of brochures do we have left?
>
> I'm not exactly sure how many boxes there are, but I think there are about seventeen.

However, that is a lot more keystrokes than "um." You might find, as many people do, that typing a long explanatory phrase takes more time than you want to spend.

Express Urgency

You have probably heard this before, but it is worth repeating: use capital letters and exclamation marks *very* sparingly. The lack of emotional cues in email makes experienced email readers hypersensitive to *any* cues that they can find. Thus, capital letters will convey the message that you are shouting. Many email users wince when they receive email like this:

```
Subject: PHROCKMEIJER ACCOUNT STATUS


HEY, I JUST WANTED TO SEE IF YOU HAD MADE ANY PROGRESS ON
THE PHROCKMEIJER ACCOUNT. STOP BY AND SEE ME SOMETIME.
```

Furthermore, upper case is hard to read. Because of the uniform height of capital letters, it takes about 10%-14% more time to read something that is entirely in uppercase than it does to read something that is in mixed case.

TIP: If you are such a poor typist that switching case is a burden for you, use all lower case instead of all upper case. It might convey the message that you're mumbling but is easier to read than all upper-case and doesn't seem as aggressive.

In Defense of Nonstandard Writing

I must warn you that there is a vocal segment that dislikes using nonstandard writing to express emotions. They argue that if Mark Twain could convey emotion without having to resort to such tricks, then we should not have to.

What they don't acknowledge is that there are big differences between Mark Twain's great novels and my electronic mail messages:

- It is flattering for someone to tell me that I should be able to write as well as Mark Twain, but not reasonable. Twain was one of the very best of the very best English-language writers. Most people sending messages are not as skilled as he was.
- Twain probably spent weeks on every chapter. I bet that he wrote, rewrote, thought, rewrote, went shopping, rewrote, went on vacation, rewrote, fixed his roof, rewrote, and rewrote some more. Twain didn't have to deal with scores of email messages every day, as many people now do.

- Twain could spend hundreds of words to convey an emotional tone. Email is usually very brief, which gives the sender less chance to convey a tone accurately.
- Books are usually written to unknown audiences, while email messages are usually to specific people—making email messages much more personal. If a male left-handed rabbit herder read a book that said nasty things about male left-handed rabbit herders, he probably wouldn't be nearly as insulted as if someone emailed him insults about male left-handed rabbit herders.

Besides, even Twain could not write to convey his tone unambiguously. When I read *Tom Sawyer* in high school, I didn't think it was funny. I naively accepted the outlandish situations.

It can be difficult to simultaneously convey emotions clearly *and* follow standard grammar rules. In the heat of the moment, one or the other is likely to suffer. While it is good to try for both, I feel that conveying emotions accurately is more important than following every grammar rule.

If You Think Someone Insulted You

You shouldn't respond angrily when you think you've been insulted. This is especially true if others are participating in the conversation. The sender might have been clumsy at expressing his or her emotion; you might have misunderstood. If you are quick to respond harshly, people might think that you have an uncontrollable temper, which usually does not lead to rapid career advancement.

If you get a piece of email that angers you, it's a good idea to take an hour to cool off. It's an even better idea to wait overnight. Re-read it later, and see if you can find a gentler interpretation. Ask a friend or colleague to look over your shoulder at the message and see if they can see another interpretation. If you decide that the message really is insulting, get a trusted person to read over your response before you send it. In a flame war, you're always better off looking like the more reasonable participant.

You'll be much better off if you send a request for clarification than an angry response:

```
Subject: Re: turtles running loose in hallway

Excuse me, I am slightly confused by your last message. I
felt that my previous message (Subject: turtles running
loose in hallway) was clear, worthwhile, and to the point.

If you meant to abuse me, could you please explain what it
was that angered you?  All that I could tell from your
previous message was that you were angry, not why.

If you meant to abuse the owner of the turtles, you want
rayman@flossrecycling.com, not me. I have never owned a
turtle.
```

An even better way to respond to inflammatory email is by talking to the person face-to-face or by telephone. You will have many more emotional cues to help you figure out the person's intent.

Summary

Emotion and meaning are more prone to misinterpretation in email messages than in more traditional communications.

- Wait before responding to a message that angers you. Have a trusted friend review any messages you wrote when you were angry.
- Convey emotions with emoticons.
- Capital letters and exclamation marks indicate urgency. Use them sparingly.
- If changing case is difficult for you, use all lower case letters instead of all uppercase letters.
- Use uncertainty markers to show how confident you are about what you say.

Make Messages Legible

What you see when you create a paper document is the same thing that your correspondent will see when reading it. On the other hand, there are a lot of different email programs, each with their own way of presenting messages. Your email program might display a message quite differently from how your correspondent's software displays it. It is relatively easy to send someone a message that they can't understand.

Why is this? For starters, when people first started using Internet email in the early 1970s, the technical and social environments were very different. Early email messages used only very simple text. Anything else would have been impractical:

- Essentially everybody using the Internet spoke English—a language with a very simple alphabet (called the "Latin character set").
- Computer-to-computer communication was very slow and expensive.
- Almost no computers had graphic display terminals.
- There was essentially no off-the-shelf software.

The first email standards didn't allow attachments, styled text, or even non-Latin character sets. Later, when people decided they wanted to be able to send more kinds of messages, the software had to stay backwards-compatible with the simple text. This means that everything sent by email today—from video to Chinese hypertext to Spanish spreadsheets—is encoded in Latin characters.

Furthermore, because the Internet grew out of a U.S. government project, it was aggressively non-profit for the first twenty years of email. No one person or company was allowed to control the email standards, so nobody could control the software. Anybody could write email software, and pretty much anybody did. (Even I have written two non-commercial email programs.) There are now many different email programs, each with different features and capabilities.

Finally, it would be impossible to make all email programs understand all file formats. In 1993 the email specification was extended to allow people to send *attachments*—documents in any arbitrary formats. However, the email program doesn't have responsibility for showing those documents. Instead, you must have "helper" programs that understand the various formats. If you don't have a helper program that understands a format, then you can't read that type of attachment.

So there are three reasons your correspondents might be unable to read your message:

- They might use an older email program that only understands plain Latin text.
- Their email program might have different capabilities than yours.
- They might not have the right helper programs to read the attachments that you send.

While your close co-workers might all use the same email program that you do, you might need to correspond with people in other divisions, other countries, or even other companies. They might not have the same email program that you do.

If you send a message that your correspondent has a hard time understanding, he or she will probably send you another message. You will then need to spend time both reading his or her message and re-writing your original message.

This section discusses the problems that might arise from a mismatch between the sending and receiving software and how to avoid having to send a message twice.

To figure out what email program your correspondent uses, open one of his or her messages in its own window, then click on the `BLAH BLAH BLAH` button in the upper left of the window. The name of the email program is usually in the `X-Mailer:` or `User-Agent:` header.

Some versions of Eudora don't use X-Mailer: or User-Agent:. However, you might be able to recognize Eudora messages from the first few characters of the Message-ID: header. A Message-ID: that starts with v, p, or a followed by four digits usually means that Eudora sent the message. (The four digits give the version number. For example, v0421 means the sender used Eudora version 4.2.1.) Message-ID: headers from Eudora for Windows frequently start with three digits, separated by periods which correspond to the version number. For example, Eudora for Windows version 4.0.1 sends messages with Message-ID: headers that start with 4.0.1.

Mozilla means Netscape Communicator; Internet Message Service usually means Microsoft Outlook.

Use Styled Text Infrequently

Most current consumer-grade email programs (including Microsoft Outlook, Microsoft Outlook Express, Netscape Communicator, and AOL) understand styled text. However, some older or more obscure email programs only understand plain text. Italics, bold, and color changes will show up to those programs as commands in the text. The sender might see something like this:

Subject: Phrockmeijer report

Hiya! Hey, I *loved* the presentation you gave to Christiaan this morning. **Great Job!**

But if the reader's software doesn't understand the formatting, the message will probably show up as something like this:

```
Subject: Phrockmeijer report
MIME-Version: 1.0
Content-type: text/html; charset="us-ascii"

<x-html><!x-stuff-for-pete base="" src="" id="0"><!doctype
html public "-//W3C//DTD W3 HTML//EN">
<html><head><style type="text/css"><!--
blockquote, dl, ul, ol, li { margin-top: 0 ; margin-bottom:
0 }
  --></style><title>Phrockmeijer report</title></
head><body>
<div><font face="Arial">Hiya!  Hey, I<i> loved</i> the
presentation you gave to Christiaan this morning. <b>
Great
Job!</b></font></div>
</body>
</html>
</x-html>
```

Keep your correspondent's capabilities in mind when you send styled text. If you don't know your correspondent's capabilities, you might want to email everything as plain text.

TIP: Even if your correspondent's email program can display styled text, you might still want to keep it simple. If you make your messages too pretty, your colleagues might think that you don't have work enough to do. They might start giving you more work or sending you jokes.

You can set Eudora to prevent you from sending styled text. Eudora will then strip all formatting out when it sends messages. To do this, go to the Tools→ Options…→Styled Text (Windows) or Special→Settings…→Styled Text (Mac OS) window and select the radio button next to Send plain text mail only.

You can also strip formatting from your message while you compose it. First, select the text you want to make plain. If you are using Eudora for Windows press

Control-Space. If you are using Eudora for Mac OS, press Command-Option-t. Alternatively, you can press the "strip formatting" button. This button is at or near the right end of the formatting toolbar, as circled in Figure 36 and Figure 37:

Figure 36: Strip Formatting Button (Mac OS)

Figure 37: Strip Formatting Button (Windows)

You can make Eudora send two messages in one, with the first part plain and the second part styled. Advanced email programs will use the styled part. People who use an older email program will see the plain, intelligible text first followed by the same kind of unintelligible text as in the previous example. To set Eudora to send both versions, select the radio button next to Send plain & styled both.

Despite the name, the button labeled Send styled mail only will only send styled text if you make some text styled (like italicized, underlined, or a different fond). Most of the time it will send plain text.

Use Default Font

People sometimes like to dress up their messages with a nicer font. I will absolutely agree that proportional-width fonts (like in this paragraph) look nicer than fixed-width fonts like this:

```
This is a fixed-width (or monospaced) font.
```

However, you need to be careful when using a proportional-width font. Even if your correspondents' software has the capability to change fonts, if that font you used isn't on their system, their software might substitute a different font. That new font probably won't have the same spacing as the font you used. Any vertical alignment that you have in your message (especially in tables) will probably get messed up.

For example, here is a message with a table that I composed in the same font as this paragraph, then converted into a monospaced font:

```
Here are my budget estimates:

Item           Jan         Feb         Mar        April
Covers         700         650         800         1930
Copying        600         525         930        1245
Folders        550         930         125          970
```

Even if your correspondents *use* an email program that can display different fonts, they might not *choose* to see different fonts. People who frequently get fonts that are too small to easily read might instruct their email program to always use their default font. Thus, what they read might not look the same as what you wrote.

TIP: To display all messages in your default font, uncheck the Font and Size boxes in Special→Settings…→Styled Text (Mac OS only).

Whitespace

Because HTML removes extra spaces and tabs, messages that are displayed in HTML might look different than the messages you composed.   This most commonly happens if your correspondent reads email through a Web-based service. The previous message can sometimes look like this when read from a Web page:

Here are my budget estimates:

Item Jan Feb Mar April
Covers 700 650 800 1930
Copying 600 525 930 1245
Folders 550 930 125 970

If you need to send tables of information to someone who reads their email with a web-based service, ask if they have a different account. If they don't, you might want to send the information in a different form.

Make Web Sites Easy to Get to

You're undoubtedly aware that Eudora recognizes URLs (the *Uniform Resource Locators* or Web addresses) in a message and makes them active. Clicking on a URL will take you to that Web location.

Unfortunately, not everyone's email program can recognize URLs. Even if your correspondent's program can, it is a lot dumber than your correspondent: the software will guess wrong sometimes. You can help the software recognize URLs correctly by taking care when writing messages.

Many email programs look for the character string `http://` to decide if something is a URL or not. If the opening `http://` isn't there, the software will think it is just regular text. This means your correspondent will have to copy the address and paste it into a Web browser by hand.

Outlook and Outlook Express will recognize URLs that start with `www` or `ftp` followed by a period. However, even Outlook and Outlook express can't recognize URLs that start with something besides `www` or `ftp`. I don't know of any email program that can recognize that these are URLs:

```
www0.mercurycenter.com
livepage.apple.com
web.nwe.ufl.edu/writing/
library.ci.sunnyvale.ca.us
sports.yahoo.com
```

It is always safer to include the `http://`!

Punctuation

While Eudora *usually* recognizes where a URL finishes and where punctuation begins, some other email software doesn't recognize the end of a URL as well.

Sometimes, email software includes any punctuation that follows the URL. For example, look at the following message:

```
Subject: URL

The URL is http://www.flossrecycling.com/phrock.html.
See if you like it!
```

Some email software thinks that the last period (after `html`) is part of the URL. Thus, if someone clicks on the link, they'll get an error that the page doesn't exist. This can lead to an unproductive email exchange, with one person insisting that the page doesn't exist and the other insisting that it does.

I will admit that it looks ugly, but it causes less confusion if there is at least a space between the URL and any punctuation:

```
Subject: URL

The URL is http://www.flossrecycling.com/phrock.html .
See if you like it!
```

You can enclose the URLs in angle brackets (<>) to make the punctuation clear:

```
Subject: URL

The URL is <http://www.flossrecycling.com/phrock.html>.
See if you like it!
```

Cut and Paste

Unfortunately, angle brackets right against the URL make it slightly harder to cut-and-paste the URL. A few years ago, I had repetitive strain injury, and had to operate a trackball with my foot. I was using an older email program that required cutting and pasting URLs, and had a really hard time getting the cursor between the < and the `http`. While I understand that not many people mouse with their feet, there are a lot of diseases that decrease coordination, making it difficult to get the cursor between the < and the `http`.

A space between the URLs and surrounding punctuation makes it much easier to select a URL:

```
Subject: URL

The URL is < http://www.flossrecycling.com/phrock.html >.
See if you like it!
```

To make cut-and-paste mindlessly easy for people, I always try to put URLs on their own lines:

```
Subject: URL

Mabel -
The URL is
        http://www.flossrecycling.com/phrock.html

See if you like it!
```

Yes, the period after the URL is now missing. While this is ungrammatical, there is no good place to put it. Fortunately, most readers don't notice that it is missing.

Long URLs

If the URL is too long or too close to the end of a line, it might get split across two lines. If that happens, most email programs usually only recognize the first line:

```
Subject: URL

Mabel -
The report is at is http://www.flossrecycling.com/phrock.
html.  See if you like it!
```

Clicking on `http://www.flossrecycling.com/phrock.` will not take Mabel to the right page!

Eudora can recognize URLs that cross lines if the URL is enclosed in angle brackets:

Subject: URL

Mabel -

The report is at is <`http://www.flossrecycling.com/phrock.`
`html`>. See if you like it!

Not all email programs are that clever, however.

If you can see that the URL is probably going to get split in two, mention that the reader might need to cut and paste both lines:

Subject: URL

The report is at is `http://www.flossrecycling.com/`
customers/phrockmeijer/2034-01-18/MeetingMinutes.html

(Note: you might need to cut and paste the above Web
address into your browser if it is too long to fit on one
line.)

TIP: If you put URLs on their own lines, they are less likely to get broken in two.

Send Attachments Infrequently

Attachments allow people to share any file in any format. GIF images, JPEG images, Word documents, WordPerfect documents, Photoshop files, Excel spreadsheets, and executable files are just a few of the types of documents people routinely attach to messages.

This can work very well: people can skim through the text of a message and save long attachments for later. However, if the reader's email software doesn't recognize attachments and receives a non-text file (like a Word document, a binary, a picture, or even compressed text), it will appear as lots of garbage. Pages and pages of garbage, usually.

Even if the readers have email software that understands what attachments are, they still need to have the right software to read the document. Think of it this way: somebody can use the Post Office to send you any kind of document. However, if someone sends you microfilm, you won't be able to read it without microfilm equipment.

Even executable programs aren't always useful to your correspondent. Macintosh programs won't run on Microsoft Windows computers; Windows 2000 programs will not run on DOS computers.

In general, it is a good idea to check with your correspondents to see what kind of attachments they can understand before sending one. Be sure to ask about version numbers and hardware platforms as well. Someone who has a Macintosh running Microsoft Word 3.0 will have difficulty opening a Word for Windows 6.0 document.

If some of your correspondents are low on disk space or have a slow Internet connection, they will not be happy to receive a large attachment—like a 200MB video—no matter how funny it is.   It is almost always better to post large documents on the Web and email the URL instead of the file. If you don't have that option, please email your correspondents first and ask if they want the attachment.

Even if your correspondent is able to view your attachments, he or she might be afraid to. You've probably already seen the problems that viruses in attachments can give an organization. Plain text messages, on the other hand, can't carry computer viruses.

Finally, it usually takes extra effort to look at an attachment. Your correspondent probably has to click on the attachment to open it, and it might take a few moments for it to show up in a window.

If you don't know what program your correspondent uses, it is almost always best to use plain text. It might be boring, but it is safe, fast, and everyone can read it.

TIP: If you are using Eudora for Windows, you should make sure that the box in Tools→Options…→Viewing Mail labeled `Allow executables in HTML content` should be UNchecked. If it's checked, you will be more vulnerable to viruses.

Word Wrap

If there is a mismatch in the line length between the sender and the receiver, the message will look ugly on the receiver's screen. Some email software will keep displaying the line until there is a carriage return, forcing the reader to scroll to the right:

```
Subject: Phrockmeijer printing quote

I've got the price quote for the report printing ready; as soon as I
```

This is ugly and difficult to read.

Eudora, like many email programs, can *word wrap*—move words to a new line if the line length is longer than the window is wide. Eudora will always word wrap incoming messages, so the previous message would be easy to read with Eudora:

```
Subject: Phrockmeijer printing quote


I've got the price quote for the report printing ready;
as soon as I get a decision on the cover selection, I'll
be ready to go.  Have you talked to the sales guys about
whether they are ready to use the blue cover or do they
want to wait and see the red one first?
```

Eudora can also wrap outgoing messages, so that your correspondents won't have to scroll to the right to read all of your messages. Eudora will wrap outgoing messages as long as you don't uncheck the box marked word wrap in Special→Settings...→Composing Mail (Mac OS) or Tools→Options...→ Composing Mail (Windows).

However, you need to be careful not to put in carriage returns at the ends of your lines. If Eudora has a different opinion of where the end of the line is, your correspondent might see alternating long lines and short lines. The break at the end of the long line will be from Eudora word wrapping; the break at the end of the short line is from the Return/Enter that you put in.

```
Subject: Phrockmeijer printing quote

I've got the price quote for the report printing ready; as
soon as I
get a decision on the cover selection, I'll be ready to go.
Have you talked
to the sales guys about whether they are ready to use the
blue
cover or do they want to wait and see the red one first?
```

The best thing to do is to leave word-wrapping enabled and let Eudora figure out where the line breaks should be. Only hit enter to start a new paragraph.

You might also sometimes see a pattern of alternating long and short lines when a message is quoted:

```
Subject: Phrockmeijer printing quote

>I've got the price quote for the report printing ready;
>as
>soon as I get a decision on the cover selection, I'll be
>ready
>to go.  Have you talked to the sales guys about whether
>they
>are ready to use the blue cover or do they want to wait
>and
>see the red one first?
```

When this person quoted the previous message, the '>' made the lines too long, so they wrapped.

Eudora will let you *unwrap* a message—remove the carriage returns and make the line lengths more uniform—but the option isn't easy to find. With Eudora for Mac OS, when you hold down the Option key, the Edit menu will change to have an option Unwrap Selection. Select the text you want to unwrap, hold down the Option key, and select Edit→Unwrap Selection.

With Eudora for Windows, highlight the text you want to unwrap and select Edit→Message Plug-ins→Unwrap Text.

You can unwrap messages that you receive as well as the ones you send, but you have to do two more steps to edit a message you received.

- Open the message in its own window.
- Click on the button in the upper left with a pencil on it, shown in Figure 38. (This lets you edit the message.)
- Unwrap the message as explained previously.

Figure 38: Pencil Button

Doing Unwrap Selection/Unwrap Text once might not improve the message as much as you want. Sometimes unwrapping again will improve the layout even more.

If, after unwrapping, you end up with '>' signs at only the beginning of each paragraph, you can try rewrapping the selection. Selecting Edit→Wrap Selection converts paragraphs that start with one '>' to a paragraph with '>' at the beginning of every line.

TIP: In addition to unwrapping a message you receive, you can strip all its formatting. Click on the pencil icon, then press Option-Command-t (Mac OS) or Control-Space (Windows).

Understand Quoting Styles

Eudora normally marks quoted material with vertical black bars—what Eudora calls *excerpt bars*—to the left of the quoted text. However, most email programs use ">". Even if you compose a message with excerpt bars, unless your correspondents use Eudora, they will probably see ">" where you see excerpt bars.

How can they see ">" when you see excerpt bars? Eudora sends the message with ">" marks at the beginning of every line of quoted material, but sends a special instruction hidden in the header. That instruction—format=flowed—tells Eudora that lines starting with ">" can be word-wrapped. When Eudora receives a message with format=flowed, it then converts the ">" marks into excerpt bars and wraps the text.

If someone is using software that doesn't understand format=flowed, the software won't translate the message. The message will have ">" at the beginning of every quoted line.

"From " at the Beginning of a Line

You need to be careful if a line in the body of a message starts with "From " (with a space after the "m". Because of some shortcuts taken when email was young and didn't know any better, "From " at the beginning of a line is always modified.

Email was traditionally stored as one long file of text, with one message after another. The first line in any email message starts with From followed by Space. (Eudora hides that line, so you won't ever see it.) Email programs could thus tell where one message stopped and the next message started by looking for "From " (with a space) at the beginning of a line.

However, if someone wrote a message that had "From " at the beginning of a line, it could fool the receiving email program into thinking that it had reached a message boundary. Thus, when sending a message, email programs are required to modify lines that start with From (with a capital F) followed by Space.

Eudora modifies lines that start with "From " by putting a space at the beginning of the line. When Eudora receives a message that starts with " From "(with Space before and after the From), it takes the space out.

Most other programs put a ">" at the beginning of lines that begin with "From ". Most programs don't remove a space in front of a From at the beginning of the line.

This means that if you are sending a message that has "From " at the beginning of a line, your correspondents might see a space that you don't. In messages that you receive, a line that starts with >From might not be a quote:

```
From: Milos Smith
To: Chantelle Williams
Subject: patent application

Dear Ms. Williams:

Pete Pittman forwarded your application to me.

At 5:37 PM, Pete Pittman said:
>Milos --
>Please review this application and let the applicants know if
>they need to provide any additional information.
>From my review, it looks fine.
```

Here, it looks like Pete Pittman is the one who thought the application was fine, not Milos Smith.

Summary

- What you see when you compose an email message is *not* always the same thing that your correspondents see when reading the message.
- If you don't know what email program your correspondent uses, it's safer to send messages as plain text.
- If your messages are too pretty, your colleagues might think you don't have enough to do.
- You can strip formatting in selected text by pressing `Control-Space` (Windows) or `Command-Option-t` (Mac OS).
- When sending a URL in email, be sure to include the `http://` part of it.
- Put URLs on lines by themselves.
- If the URL is long enough that it will cross lines, put angle brackets (<>) around it and/or warn your correspondent that they might have to cut and paste multiple lines.
- Avoid all punctuation except for angle brackets (<>) right before or after URLs.
- Some email software doesn't understand attachments at all. Your attachments will then show up as pages and pages of garbage.
- Even when your correspondent's email software can decode attachments, your correspondent might not have the right software to view it. It's a good idea to check with your correspondent to see what format (including version numbers!) he or she can read before sending an attachment.
- Even if your correspondent has an application that can read an attachment, he or she might not want to open it. Helper programs can take a little while to start up and attachments sometimes have computer viruses.
- People with slow Internet connections or limited disk space might be annoyed if you send them large attachments. It is almost always better to post large files on a local network or the Web and send only the URL.
- Turn word wrapping *on* and let Eudora figure out where to put the line breaks. Only type `enter` to start a new paragraph.

CHAPTER 10

Get and Keep Attention

Picture your correspondent. She's sitting at a desk in a noisy office. She's right under the cooling duct, so she's cold. She's wearing glasses that are two years out of date and has to lean forward to read her screen. Her neck is sore. She's read fifty messages today and has another fifty in her inbox. She's tired, and to top it off, she's hungry. She wants to go home.

Why should she read your message?

If you don't grab her attention, she might never get around to reading your message. You will then need to send her another piece of email (which she also might not read), chase her down in person, or phone her. What a waste of time!

If you don't *keep* her attention, she might not read your message carefully and completely. She might skim over a key point and so not address it. Worse, she might abandon the message before finishing. Again, you would have to waste some of your time to get the response you need. Thus, it is a good idea to call attention to important messages.

You should also tell the truth about messages that are *not* important. If you routinely exaggerate the importance of your messages, your correspondents won't believe you when you write a message that really *is* important. If, on the other hand, you always show when messages have low priority, you will gain credibility with your correspondents. They'll be more likely to respond to your important messages.

This chapter shows techniques for quickly conveying a message's importance and main points. In turn, this will help you get and keep your correspondents' attention, allowing you to work more efficiently.

Get Attention

To get attention, you must make your purpose known quickly. If you waste your correspondents' time, you're not likely to get what you need when you need it. Ideally, your correspondents should be able to figure out what you want within the first few lines of your message.

Get Attention with Subject Headers

The first chance you have to get your correspondents' attention is in the subject header of your message. A clear indication of a message's topic and urgency will help your message stand out in your correspondents' (possibly long) list of messages. Subject: headers should summarize the message compactly, with the most important ideas at the beginning.

If you have trouble coming up with a good subject, imagine walking up to your correspondent and saying, "I'd like to talk to you about…" or "I'd like to ask you about…" The words that complete the sentence will probably make a good subject.

Signal Words

You might already be using some high-impact words or abbreviations in subject lines to signal your intentions.

The words URGENT:, REQ:, ACTION REQUIRED:, CAUTION:, or DANGER: in subject lines will—unless you overuse them—call attention to your messages. Putting the signal words BTW:, FYI:, and HUMOR: in the subject line of your low-priority messages will make your *other* messages look more important by contrast. (See "Signal Words and Abbreviations in the Subject" on page 225, for more on common signal words.)

Because it might not be immediately obvious if a message is going only to one person or to many, you might be able to get more attention by using your correspondent's name in the subject lines:

```
Subject: Mabel: budget estimates
```

Occasionally, the message will be so short that it will fit completely on the Subject: line. In such cases, you can end the Subject: line with EOM or eom, for End Of Message.

```
Subject: red minivan lights on, license 2DLH822(EOM)
```

Don't forget to repeat the contents of the subject line in the body of the message, as mentioned in "Repeat Subject in the Body" on page 161.

TIP: Because not everybody understands EOM, you might want to spell out End of Message in the body of the message.

Signal Importance with Addressing Method

Which distribution option you choose—To:, Cc:, or Bcc:—can tell your correspondents how you hope they will respond to the message.

To:

You should use the To: header for people who the message affects directly. This includes people who:

- have specifically requested information contained in your message,
- might know the answer to a question in your message, or
- you would like to take an action in response to your message.

Putting people on the To: header encourages them to respond.

Cc:

If you do *not* want a response unless something is wrong, you can use Cc: This lets people stay informed but tells them that they don't need to respond, leading to less email for you. There are several reasons why you would add a group of people to the Cc: list:

- You think that one or more of the Cc: group might have comments or corrections. You might be paraphrasing something one of the Cc: group said, or you might be less of an authority than someone in the Cc: group.
- You think the outcome of the conversation will affect the Cc: group (but they won't have to take any direct action).
- You think the Cc: group needs to know the information in the message. (For example, your boss might want to know what you're up to.)

Here is an example of a message that uses To: and Cc: well:

```
To: jim@flossrecycling.com
Cc: john@flossrecycling.com, betsy@flossrecycling.com,
    donald@flossrecycling.com, charles@flossrecycling.com,
    maryjane@flossrecycling.com
From: liz@flossrecycling.com
Subject: Release 3.1.4.2

Jim -
I've attached the change orders for Release 3.1.4.2. I've
checked with John, Betsy, Donald, Charles, and Mary Jane,
and they say they are ready to ship just as soon as you
approve the change orders. Please review and approve the
change orders as soon as you can.
```

Here Jim was the only one who needed to take an action as a result of the message, so he was the only one on the To: header. John, Betsy, Donald, Charles, and Mary Jane did not have actions that they needed to perform, so Liz did not put them on the To: header. Liz put the other people in the Cc: header, so they wouldn't need to respond but could make corrections if Liz misunderstood something.

TIP: Don't add high-status people who are not genuinely involved in your issue. Your status will suffer if a high-status people replies to everybody with, "Who are you and why are you sending me this?"

Bcc:/Group Nicknames with Full Name

As mentioned in Chapter 5, *Reduce the Number of Incoming Messages*, nobody can see your `Bcc:` list except you. Group nicknames that have Full Names also hide the list of receivers, as discussed in "How to Use Group Nicknames to Discourage Discussions" on page 125. Using `Bcc:` or a named group nickname means that responses to your message will only go to you.

If you think that your correspondents will want to read your message but not any later discussion, you should use `Bcc:` or a named group nickname. This is not only nice for your correspondents but also useful to you. The fewer messages your correspondents get from other people, the more time they will have for messages from you.

Use Your Correspondent's Name

If you greet your correspondent by name in the body of the message, then you've made it clear that the message is specifically for him or her. Your correspondent will know that you are not sending your message to an arbitrary group of people in the hope that someone—anyone—in the group will answer it.

If you are addressing a group instead of an individual, you can use a functional name in the greeting, like `Dear Payroll Data-Entry Clerks`. Even such an impersonal greeting tells each of the payroll data-entry clerks that the message might be of interest to them.

Yes, the address list can show how many people you sent the message to, but people don't always look at the address lists. If you put your correspondent's name in the body of the message, you make it obvious.

Identify Yourself to Strangers

People who don't know you are much more likely to pay attention to your message if they have an idea of what you want and who you are. You should get their attention by answering the following questions very quickly:

- Who are you? In what role are you acting?
- How did you hear of your correspondent?
- Why will your correspondent be interested in your message?

Do this at the beginning of the message. It should not take more than three or four lines. Frequently, it will take only one sentence to answer all three questions. For example:

```
Subject: playground tour
To: Mabel Garcia <mabel@flossresearch.com>
From: J. Wilson <tallperson@catfloss.org>

Mabel -

Ezra Snodwhistle said that you were interested in getting a
tour of the rose garden that I designed.

Ezra said you would like to see it before the Rose
Gardeners' Club meeting on Tuesday, 19 Jan 2038, at 4 PM.
I'd be happy to show you the garden, but I have to take my
horse to the dentist that day at 3 PM.  If you have time, I
can show you the garden after the meeting.
```

Giving your name isn't as important as explaining your role. Your name alone probably doesn't help your correspondents figure out the message's topic.

Use Priority Levels

Eudora allows you to mark the priority of a message. This can be a useful attention-getter.

However, you should not rely too heavily on priority levels for getting attention.

- Different email software programs implement priority signals differently. Some of your correspondents might not be able to see the priorities you set.
- Many people ignore priority levels because too many people set the priority level higher than their messages deserve.
- Filters can reset the priority level.

If you do mark messages' priorities, be realistic. If you mark all of your messages high-priority, people will stop trusting your ratings. You should mark no more than ten percent of your messages with the highest priority. Conversely, you should be careful to give low priority to messages that are not very urgent or important. If you consistently give your messages appropriate priority levels, your correspondents might learn to trust your priority ratings.

Mark priorities for messages according to how important they are to *your correspondents*, not to *you*. That your child scored well on an exam might be the most important thing in the world to you, but it is unlikely that anyone else at your workplace will like being interrupted to learn that.

Also be sensitive to your status in your organization's hierarchy. If you send something with highest priority to your subordinates, they will give it more attention than if it came from a peer. Your subordinates might suddenly stop everything to handle a high-priority message from you. On the other hand, your boss might be irritated by a message that calls too loudly for his or her attention.

Keep Attention

Getting attention is not very useful if you can't keep it. This is not a trivial task. Your correspondents undoubtedly want to deal with your message as quickly as possible. You need to make the message easy to read, make your points easy to find, and present yourself as someone worth responding to.

Make the Message Easy to Read

Your correspondents want to get through your messages as fast as possible. Help them.

Shorten the Message

Most email messages are part of ongoing negotiations so do not need to be very long. Whenever possible, keep your message short enough that your correspondents don't need to scroll to see all of it. When reading a long message, they might decide that the delete button is easier to reach than the scrollbar.

Granted, if your document is a report or plan whose purpose is to give extensive detail—like an annual report or a marketing campaign plan—it might need to be long. In such cases, sending it by email might not be the best way to distribute it. If you have the capability, it is better to post long documents on a Web page and send only its Web address. Besides keeping the email message short, this lets you make changes to the document after you send out the Web address.

If you are sending a message to a lot of people, a named group nickname helps to shorten the message. It can be annoying to have to wade through all the addresses to get to the body of the message.

If you don't want to create a group nickname with a `Full Name`, you can use `Bcc:` and put a line in your message somewhere that summarizes who you are sending the message to:

```
(Bcc used to trim the address list; this message sent to 50
of Mabel's most intimate friends)
```

You can also use the greeting to show who else is getting the message:

```
Subject: birthday party!

Dear friends of Mabel's:

Mabel's 45th birthday is coming up soon. I am planning on
having a party for her at Mama Del's Pizza Parlor next
Saturday, June 6th, at 6 PM. Please join us!
```

Because hiding the addresses can be a signal that the receivers don't need to respond, you might want to say explicitly if you want the unnamed people to respond:

```
Subject: birthday party!

Dear friends of Mabel's:

Mabel's 45th birthday is coming up soon. I am planning on
having a party for her at Mama Del's Pizza Parlor next
Saturday, June 6th, at 6 PM. Please join us!

Please tell me if you can come or not.
```

Shorten Paragraphs

You should keep your paragraphs short, not just your messages. It is easier to locate a sentence that is near the beginning or ending of a paragraph, so shorter paragraphs make it easier for your correspondents to find their places. While this is true when reading any text, it is especially useful when your readers scroll through text. The somewhat unpredictable jumping of scrolled text makes it even easier for readers to lose their place. Keeping paragraphs short reduces the chance that a reader will skip a sentence or two.

Avoid Attachments

As mentioned in Chapter 9, *Make Messages Legible*, not everybody can read all attachments. Even if your correspondents can open attachments, they might not want to. In addition to potentially exposing your correspondence to viruses, opening attachments can take a few moments that your correspondents might not want to spare. You are more likely to keep their attention with a plain, text-based message.

Make Your Points Easy to Find

Making it easier for your correspondents to track the text is good, but you also need to make your points easy to find.

Cut Extraneous Information

One of the fastest ways to lose your readers is to hide the point of the message. In the example below, the real reason for sending the message is hidden in the middle of a huge amount of irrelevant material:

```
Subject: information
```

Dear Ms. Garcia:

I'm a nurse at the Medical Center of Carp (East Wing) in Indiana. I have two dogs, three kids, and a fabulous wife who comes from Paris, Illinois. She's also named Mabel, and her maiden name was Garcia, too! Quite a coincidence, huh? My business manager is really hassling me about my floss budget. He's a bit of a jerk, but I can't quit now, so I have to put up with it. How much floss per patient is reasonable? I have been using about 10 cm per patient per night. I guess I can see how hospital spending could get cut, what with HMOs and all. That doesn't mean I have to like it. My wife is pretty good at stretching our limited budget. For example, she has this great recipe for fake Cornish game hens that is so good that it doesn't matter what the price of real hens is. Would you like the recipe?

Your correspondents could easily get bored with a message like this and not read it carefully, postpone reading it, or ignore it completely. This means more work for you to get the response you need.

You are much more likely to get speedy responses with a message like this:

```
Subject: typical floss usage
```

Dear Ms. Garcia -

I'm wondering what reasonable floss consumption in a hospital setting is. I'm using approximately 10 centimeters per patient per night. How much floss do most hospitals use?

Put the Most Important Topic First

If you introduce topics in the order of their importance, your correspondent will find the main point right away. It's also a good idea to mark non-essential text with the phrases "for your information" (FYI) or "by the way" (BTW). That way, your correspondent has a clearer idea of what points you care most about:

```
Subject: typical floss usage

Dear Ms. Garcia -

I'm wondering what reasonable floss consumption in a
hospital setting is. I'm using approximately 10
centimeters per patient per night. How much floss do most
hospitals use?

BTW, my wife is also named Mabel, and her maiden name was
Garcia! Quite a coincidence, huh? She's from Paris,
Illinois, a wonderful mother to our two dogs and three
kids, and a great cook. She's got an outstanding recipe for
fake Cornish game hens, for example. Would you like
the recipe?
```

Discuss One Issue per Message

Once your correspondents have found your main point, you need to make sure they don't lose it again. Sending a message with several unrelated issues that need a response can lead to trouble. It is easy for your correspondent to discuss only one of the points raised, forgetting the others. It's even fairly common for people to neglect the most important issue, as in this example:

```
Subject: Re: typical floss usage

>Dear Ms. Garcia -
>
>I'm wondering what reasonable floss consumption in a
>hospital setting is. I'm using approximately 10
>centimeters per patient per night. How much floss do most
> hospitals use?
>
>BTW, my wife is also named Mabel, and her maiden name was
>Garcia! Quite a coincidence, huh? She's from Paris,
>Illinois, a wonderful mother to our two dogs and three
>kids, and a great cook. She's got an outstanding recipe
>for fake Cornish game hens, for example. Would you like
>the recipe?

I love Cornish game hens! I would love to have that recipe.
```

Long messages are more vulnerable to this problem than short messages: what scrolls off the screen frequently scrolls out of short-term memory. Topics that require thought or a lot of research are also likely to make your reader forget previous topics.

You should try to limit your email messages to a single topic or set of closely related topics. While it is cumbersome to send two separate paper letters for two topics, addressing and sending email is so fast that sending multiple messages in succession should not be a burden.

If you are worried that your correspondents will feel overwhelmed if they get a lot of messages from you all at once, ask yourself if you would rather get one long message or several short messages. If it still bothers you to send multiple messages, put a note in the first message that warns them that further messages are coming.

Summarize Long Messages at the Beginning and End

If you insist on sending a message that raises multiple issues, summarize the issues at the beginning of the message. Then, at the end of the message, mention each of the issues again. This is particularly important if there are questions that you need answered. For example:

Subject: staff meeting issues

Chantelle,

Yesterday's staff meeting brought up three issues: interns, the picnic, and the patent application.

First, the summer is approaching quickly, and we need to figure out how many interns we want. Jeff has already asked for an intern to help with the paper clip inventory, but I think we can get two more. Do you have any unpleasant tasks that a student could do?

Second, the Picnic Committee is still looking for a good place for the summer party. I remember your husband raving about the place his company's picnic was held a few years ago - that place where the geese stole his boss' toupee. Can you remember the name of that place?

Third, Martha Boise in Legal is ready to start working on your patent application. As soon as you and Winston have finished with the budget estimates, I'd like you to give the patent application your full attention.

So:
+ Where do you think summer interns would be useful?
+ Where was your husband's company picnic?
+ When will you and Winston finish the budget estimates?

The way this message is structured, Chantelle isn't likely to forget to answer any of the questions.

Separate Quotes with Blank Lines

White space is very helpful for making the boundaries between quoted and new material clear. Eudora will automatically insert a blank line, but it is possible to delete the line between old and new.

If quoted and new material runs together, your correspondent might skip over one of your points, thinking it was part of a quote. If Mabel reads the following message quickly, she might miss the line in the middle. Mabel might think that Chantelle agreed to finish the budget estimates by Thursday:

```
Subject: Re: budget estimates
To: Mabel Garcia <mabel@flossresearch.com>
From: Chantelle Williams <chantelle@flossresearch.com>
```

> Are you going to have the budget estimates printed up and
> distributed by Thursday? Pat wants everything by Friday.
No, I haven't gotten the sales results from Winston yet.
> Additionally, I'd like it if you would please order seven
> reports with blue covers (not yellow) for the Expo.
I can do that.

If your correspondents don't use Eudora, they will probably see ">" instead of the black vertical bars. It is even easier to misread messages with ">" quotes:

```
Subject: Re: budget estimates
To: Mabel Garcia <mabel@flossresearch.com>
From: Chantelle Williams <chantelle@flossresearch.com>
```

>Are you going to have the budget estimates printed up and
>distributed by Thursday? Pat wants everything by Friday.
No, I haven't gotten the sales results from Winston yet.
>Additionally, I'd like it if you would please order seven
>reports with blue covers (not yellow) for the Expo.
I can do that.

A blank line separating quotes and next text makes the message much more legible.

It is also helpful to put *two* blank lines between the end of a section of new material and the start of another quote. The second blank line shows that you are done discussing the first quote and have moved on to the second quote:

```
Subject: Re: budget estimates
To: Mabel Garcia <mabel@flossresearch.com>
From: Chantelle Williams <chantelle@flossresearch.com>

Are you going to have the budget estimates printed up and
distributed by Thursday? Chris wants everything by Friday.

No, I haven't gotten the sales results from Winston yet.


Additionally, I'd like it if you would please order seven
reports with blue covers (not yellow) for the Expo.

I can do that.
```

Chapter 9, *Make Messages Legible*, discusses in detail a number of other issues affecting legibility of messages.

Shorten Quotes

Electronic mail messages frequently contain material quoted from previous messages. There are good reasons for quoting material, as discussed in "Provide Adequate Context" on page 156. However, quotes that are too long or too hard to follow will make your correspondent lose interest and/or miss your point.

When you incorporate a long original message into a response, your response is more readable when you remove extraneous text and/or paraphrase the original message. This makes it easy for your reader to find your points. For example,

Chantelle could respond to the message on page 207 by quoting only the last three lines:

```
Subject: Re: staff meeting issues
To: Mabel Garcia <mabel@flossrecycling.com>
From: Chantelle Williams <chantelle@flossrecycling.com>
─────────────────────────────────────────────────────

>+ Where do you think summer interns would be useful?

It would be really nice to have someone to keep the break
rooms tidy and the coffee pots full.


>+ Where was your husband's company picnic?

It was held out at Land O'Clowns, but I can't recommend it.
It was cold, windy, and the geese stole all the hot dog
buns.


>+ When will you and Winston finish the budget estimates?

Tomorrow, I hope. Winston's creeping Norwegian sunwarts
have stopped itching enough that he's able to concentrate
again.
```

You should quote only enough context to make the message clear. Try to keep quoted material to less than half of the lines in an email message.

With Eudora, it is easy to create a reply with just the text you want to include. With Eudora for Mac OS, you need to select the text that you want, then hold down the Shift key while selecting Reply. A new reply composition window will appear with only the text you selected, with that text properly quoted. This works regardless of how you select Reply:

- clicking on the Reply button
- typing Command-r
- selecting Message→Reply

With Eudora for Windows, if you have selected any text, replying usually quotes only the text you selected. You can change to quoting the entire message by selecting `Tools`→`Option…`→`Replying` and unchecking the box next to `Quote only the selected text`.

If you don't have time to edit a quote and must include the whole thing, put your comments *before* the quote. Paging through a long quote to get to your comments might irritate your readers.

TIP: Many people quote the entire message, no matter how long. If you shorten quotes, you will have less to read through when your correspondents quote your message back at you.

Raise Your Perceived Status

The higher your perceived status, the more interested people will be in reading (and finishing) your message. However, your correspondents can't tell much about who you are from email.

Your correspondents will probably do the same thing you might catch yourself doing—make assumptions on the flimsiest of pretexts. I am emphatically *not* saying that people *should* stereotype, just trying to warn you that they *might*.

Language

Your language probably influences people's impression of your status more than anything else. Lots of misspellings, poor grammar, and misused words will make people suspect that you are uneducated. From that, they might conclude that you are not very clever. It doesn't matter that the correlation between language skill and intelligence is weak (especially among non-native speakers); many people will draw that conclusion anyway.

Some people are literally insulted by messages that contain errors, especially typographical errors. They feel that flagrant errors show disrespect: if you cared, you would have been more careful.

Eudora in Paid or Sponsored mode has a built-in spelling checker and fixer. For every word that is <u>underlined</u> (Mac OS) or <u>double-underlined</u> (Windows), Eudora can suggest a better spelling. To see Eudora's suggestions under Mac OS, `Control`-click on a misspelled word. Under Windows, right-click on the misspelled word.

Show Status Explicitly

You can influence people's impressions by showing your status explicitly. You can do this by adding a signature that shows your job title:

```
Subject: catalog request
From: Martha Boise <marty@flossresearch.com>

Please email me information about your product line.

--
Martha J. Boise
Vice-President of Legal Affairs
Floss Recycling Incorporated
```

Your signature should be brief. Your name is probably in the message header and your email address always is. To reply by email, your correspondent probably doesn't even need to look at your email address. You should only give your phone number and address if you are willing to get phone calls and visitors!

TIP: A signature sends a signal to your readers that they have read your entire message. If you don't routinely sign messages, people might accidentally stop after the first page of a two-page message. They are less likely to forget to scroll if they are used to seeing your signature at the end.

It can also be effective to start your message with status information:

```
Subject: catalog request

Hi, I'm the Vice-President of Legal Affairs at Floss
Recycling Incorporated. Please email me information about
your product line; I'm interested in buying your company.
```

Personal Opinion on Language

I have read a number of "email etiquette" guides that say that you should always use correct grammar and spelling, as if the etiquette authority wants you to stop deliberately inserting errors. Nobody wants their messages to have errors, but it takes time and effort to double-check a message. If you write forty messages every day, you might not have the time to make every message perfect.

I have known some people who are paralyzed by their perfectionism. They worry so much about getting everything right that they never send *any* messages. I would much rather quickly get a response with errors than never get a perfect one. If you don't respond to my messages, I will think less of you than if you don't conjugate your verbs properly.

If you only have a limited amount of time to spend on a message to me, I'd prefer that you spend your time on making sure there is adequate context than on making your grammar flawless. I'd much rather get a message that says:

```
Subject: Warning!

There is 50 people with machine guns on Main Street abt 1
mi aways wallking north and they not friendly so getcher
selves outta here protno!!!!!
```

than one about the same situation that says:

```
Subject: Warning!
─────────────────────────────────────────────
You would be advised to leave the building promptly.
```

I can usually guess what the proper grammar is; I usually can't guess what the proper context is.

Choosing Your Battles

How much energy should you invest in raising your perceived status for a particular message? That depends upon several things:

- Do you know your correspondents already? Your message probably won't change the opinions of the people you work most closely with, but if you are sending a message to someone in another division who you've never met, you probably want to mention what your job function is.
- What depends on the mail? If you are sending email to the head of your organization, you probably should be careful about your grammar. Salespeople who want your business, on the other hand, are paid to not care about your grammar.
- Are your correspondents likely to care? The head of the documentation department might care more about your spelling than your project team leader. People who send lots of email will probably be more tolerant than people who have the luxury of spending an hour on every email message.
- What do your correspondents' messages look like? If they send you email with incorrect punctuation, poor spelling, and bad grammar, they probably won't care too much if you do the same.

Get and Keep Attention

Summary

To get attention:

- Write compelling subject headers that are compact and summarize your messages.
- Put signal words in subject headers: URGENT:, REQ:, ACTION REQUIRED:, CAUTION!, DANGER!, and first names are useful to raise priority. FYI: and BTW: are useful for conveying that a message is less urgent.
- If you can keep the message to one line, put it in the Subject: line. Use eom at the end of the subject to show that there is no further information (but be sure to repeat the information in the body of the message!)
- Use To: for people who you want to take an action. Use Cc: for people who are interested, affected, or authorities. Use Bcc: to shorten address lists, maintain privacy, and spare your correspondents from follow-up discussions.
- Use priority levels, but only mark things urgent if they really are. Always show when a message is low-priority.
- Identify yourself to strangers and explain why you chose to write to them.

To keep attention:

- Make your messages and paragraphs short: scrolling is hard.
- Cut information that isn't essential. Shorten long quotes, paraphrasing or deleting as needed.
- Put topics in order of importance.
- If you need to write about unrelated issues, try to put them in different messages.
- If a message is long or contains several unrelated topics, summarize the message at both the beginning and the end.
- Use blank lines between quoted material to improve legibility.
- When asking for a favor, show that you've already put some effort into solving the problem.
- Raise your perceived status with proper grammar and spelling or by explicitly giving your position.

CHAPTER 11

Improve Your Company's Email Effectiveness

Changing your own behavior—filtering, using pre-written responses, writing good subject lines, providing adequate context, and so forth—will make getting through your email much easier. However, at some point, you will be limited by how well your company deals with email.

Your company's email behaviors might have been the result of conscious decisions, but it's more likely that its culture evolved spontaneously. Your company can probably improve its email effectiveness.

There are three basic ways to change behavior in an company: improve resources, provide training, and set policy. This chapter will discuss each method and suggest specific examples of each that can help improve email efficiency.

Improve Resources

Providing good resources can make desirable behaviors easier and undesirable behaviors harder or impossible. Technology is one powerful resource for changing behavior. Unfortunately, technological changes almost always cost money—to buy (or develop), configure, and maintain the software.

If you are technically proficient, you might be able to influence your company's email usage by developing one or more of the following resources.

Web-based Mailing List Interface

If your company sets up mailing lists for different functional groups, your company will be more productive. Not only do mailing lists make it easy to send messages to the right people, they make filtering extremely easily. This improves people's ability to organize and prioritize.

Making it easy for people to set up mailing lists is thus good for the company. Something that works well is to have a web-based interface to mailing lists with information on

- what lists are available
- what their policies are
- who the "owner" of the list is
- who has subscribed
- how to subscribe
- how to unsubscribe

A searchable Web-based archive with all the messages from a list is also very useful.

- An archive helps people who delete a message and then decide later that they wanted to see it.
- It is easier to catch up after an absence if the mailing list messages are in an archive.
- An archive is a useful resource for training new employees.
- An archive creates a record of what decisions were made and why.
- People are sometimes a bit more polite and careful if they know that their comments are stored.

External Subscribers

Letting people from outside the company subscribe to mailing lists has benefits and disadvantages. If your company allows people from outside the company to be on a mailing list, employees can send confidential information outside the company accidentally. (Because senders don't see who is on a list when they mail to it, it is easy to make that mistake.) On the other hand, if your company does not allow external subscribers, then nobody can set up lists of customers and vendors that you might want to correspond with in bulk. One compromise

Improve Your Company's Email Effectiveness

solution is to have a privileged set of people who can create and maintain mailing lists with both internal and external subscribers.

Your company might also want to have a different naming convention for internal-only and internal/external lists. That way, people can see quickly how confidential messages to the list are.

Geographical Mailing Lists

There should be a mailing list for every geographical area so that messages that apply only to one location don't also go to other locations. The classic example of what happens if you don't have this is everyone worldwide getting messages like this:

```
Subject: blue Ford 2RSM183 - headlights on
```

Facilities closures, maintenance, and party announcements are frequently mis-addressed as well.

Once your company has geographic mailing lists, training can impress upon people that they shouldn't waste people's time by sending to the wrong list. Peer pressure can keep people from making that mistake twice.

Reply-to-All vs. Reply-to-Sender

Mailing list servers should be configured so that the From: header has the author of the message, not the listname address. This will ensure that simple replies (including out-of-office messages) go to just the original author, not the whole list. (It would be nice if people wouldn't send automatic responses to mailing lists, but the more people you have on a list, the more likely that someone will make that mistake.)

Security

Email attachments can contain viruses. Hopefully, everyone will have the latest virus-checking software on their desktop computer. However, people are lazy. Unfortunately, if one person fails to install the latest virus-checker, that can affect the entire company. It is slower but safer to check all attachments automatically before the receivers have a chance to see them.

Certain types of attachments are more prone to viruses than others. In particular, executable files (with extension .exe) can be deadly, and are rarely useful. Your company might wish to delete all .exe attachments that come from outside the company.

Eliminate Duplicates

If your company's mailing list software can remove redundant copies of messages, that can save people a lot of aggravation. There are times when a message is appropriate for several different mailing lists. If people subscribe to multiple lists, however, that means they could get multiple copies of the same message—which gets dull quickly. Sending each person only one copy of a message will help people get through their email faster.

Develop a Good Web Site

A good Web site for your company or department means that people can refer their correspondents to information on a Web page instead of creating it all themselves. For example, if your company has a Web page with a map and directions to its location, people won't have to spend time writing directions. They can instead send the URL of the map.

Any sort of information that people ask about regularly is helpful to put on a Web site. These include things like benefit details, lists of medical providers, technical specifications, company charts, and even floorplans.

Develop Corporate- or Department-Wide Responses

It might save time for someone in the company to carefully develop stationery for common questions, then make them available to the whole company. For example, a non-profit might make a mission statement available. A corporation might want to have a blurb directing people to the public relations department:

```
I'm sorry, I really am not the appropriate person to
discuss this with. You need to talk to Sal Mgabi in our
Public Relations department. His phone number is +1-217-
555-7777x77.
```

A Customer Support department might have a large number of canned responses that would be useful to have easily available, like:

```
The problem of the Harik Quicksilver Electric Bagpipes
overheating has been fixed in release 3.1.4.1.5.9. To
download the patch, go to
<http://www.electricbagpipes.com/harik/rel314159.zip>

The overheating is only a problem if all the drones are
blocked. Keeping the drones clear will prevent this
problem.

Should you have any further questions, please do not
hesitate to ask.
```

Good Email Software

Eudora is an excellent general-purpose email program. However, for people doing customer support, Customer Relationship Management software might be better.

Customer Relationship Management (abbreviated CRM or eCRM) software makes it easier to keep track of and use a company's pre-written responses. While these are most useful for customer support personnel, they can also be useful for anybody who gets many routine questions.

I have found that an "auto-suggest" filter action is extremely useful. I was able to get through messages about ten times faster when I had a system that let me select (with one click) from several suggested responses. I could then, if I chose, edit the response(s) before sending them.

This isn't as fast as responding completely automatically, but allowing a human being to make the choices cuts down on the number of inappropriate responses. Humans are still a lot smarter than computers.

Most CRM software will also allow you to track all communication that you have had with the sender of the incoming message. Again, this is most useful for support personnel, but anybody who manages a lot of communications—like people in sales or fund raising—could find it useful.

Provide Alternatives to Distracting Messages

People, left to their own devices, will generate all kinds of messages that are not directly related to work. Some of the most common non-work messages are about

- goods to buy, sell or give away (for example, "spare ticket to Monday's football game")
- requests for recommendations of products or services
- jokes
- notification that food is available (for example, "leftover bread and cheese in conference room C4")
- notification that automobile headlights are on

Eliminating these messages might be difficult and create bad will. What your company can do, however, is create better channels for sending non-essential messages, as I describe below.

Mailing Lists

If you set up specific mailing lists for the distracting messages, then people can filter them into low-priority mailboxes. For example, a mailing list for leftover food would be easy to filter.

Web-based Services

Another, more sophisticated, option is to set up web-based services. For example, your company could set up a simple Web-based application that would send mail *only* to the owner of the car whose lights are on. (People would have to enter their license plate numbers, but their reward for doing so is high.) Your company might also provide Web-based applications that tell where to find leftover food, a marketplace, and a place to review products and services.

Where Are Your Colleagues?

Another useful Web-based application is one that lets employees check in and check out of the office. Then people can use the Web application to find out where someone is. This is better than having coworkers send email to everybody whenever they leave the office: those who don't care that someone is gone won't have to read a message about it.

Out-of-Office Messages

Sometimes, casual users can set up their email system to automatically respond to incoming messages with a "out-of-office" message:

```
Subject: out of the office until 29 Feb

I am at the Floss Expo in Fargo, ND and will not be
returning until 29 Feb. I will be checking my voicemail on
a daily basis. If you need immediate assistance, please
contact Chantelle Williams at x2202.
```

However, casual users usually set up their out-of-office messages to respond to ALL incoming messages. This means that anybody who sends a message to a mailing list frequently gets back several out-of-office messages. If both the sender and receiver have out-of-office messages, their email programs can get into a loop where they keep telling each other that they are out of the office. Additionally, people sometimes forget to turn their out-of-office messages off.

Given all that, it is a good idea to set up a Web-based application that configures out-of-office messages so that

- only one message per absence (or per week) goes to any individual account
- out-of-office messages don't go to mailing lists (or perhaps to *any* external accounts)
- bounce messages don't generate a out-of-office message
- messages that contain the phrases "vacation" or "out of the office" don't generate a out-of-office message.
- out-of-office messages stop automatically at the scheduled end of the absence

Filters

It is very valuable for the company to set up filters that remove unsolicited commercial email before it gets anywhere close to the end user. Junk email can take up an enormous amount of time and energy.

While the filters inn Chapter 3 are good starting points for filters, having a set of pre-made filters might help your company's productivity. Your company could then customize the filters for its specific situation. Employees could use the pre-made filters as guides in developing their own.

Confidential Material

Email makes it very easy to transmit confidential material, but email has very poor security. Anything highly confidential should be sent via a trusted courier. One way to make it more difficult to disclose confidential information is to have a computer program examine all outgoing messages for a set of words marking confidentiality. For example, Mabel's company could prevent people from emailing documents containing the phrase `Floss Recycling Inc. Confidential`.

Messages from the Company

From time to time, someone will need to send a message to the entire company about policy changes, facilities closures, and so on. For large companies, it can be dangerous to send that message from a personal account. The sender might get hundreds of messages from employees. (If nothing else, there could be a lot of out-of-office messages.) On the other hand, if updates come from an email address that is not attached to a person, it can seem very cold and impersonal.

One way around this is to make the message from an impersonal address, but to give the name of the person who sent the message. Then ask that follow-up comments go to a web-based discussion forum. Ask that people not post messages unless they have something new to add, but add a way to count "I like this" or "I don't like this" votes.

Provide Training

Many of the tools above *enforce* good practice, but good training can *encourage* good practices. If your company does not have the technical resources to develop tools like the above, adding training on email effectiveness can be valuable.

Even if your company has the time, money, and skill to develop resources, training might be useful. Good resources won't help everything; in particular, technical aids do a poor job of helping people write more understandable messages.

Training is particularly productive if the unwanted behavior is the result of uninformed or unconscious decisions. Showing the benefits of doing things a different way might be all that it takes to change the behavior.

If your company can come to agreement on what behaviors are acceptable, peer pressure can enforce those behaviors. If five hundred people all reply, "that wasn't appropriate" to an unacceptable message, the sender isn't likely to make that mistake again. To make this work, however, the culture must accept or encourage this type of vigilante justice.

The disadvantage of training everybody is that it takes time and energy—which usually means money.

Signal Words and Abbreviations in the Subject

Even if your company doesn't have the resources to make more appropriate homes for distracting messages, it can get similar results if everybody uses the same signal words in `Subject:` headers. If people use the signal words consistently, those who are not interested in a certain type of message can filter them into low-priority mailboxes or delete them outright. Examples of useful signal words are:

- OT: for messages that are Off-Topic—not directly related to a mailing list's topic
- REQ: for REQuest—meaning the sender wants the receiver to do something
- LIGHTS: for messages about cars whose headlights are on
- FOOD: for messages that there is leftover food available for the taking
- WHERE: to notify people of a temporary absence
- OOO: for automatic responses that the sender is out of the office
- FS: for messages advertising something For Sale
- WTB: for messages expressing a desire to purchase something (Wanted To Buy)
- EOM to show that the subject line contains the entire message
- TC: for Time Critical

It doesn't really matter what words people use, as long as everybody uses them consistently. Your company will be just fine if everybody uses AR: (for Action Request) instead of REQ:. But if some people use AR:, some use REQ:, some use AI:, and some use DIRECTIVE:, it will be harder for people to set up filters.

Training can also reduce confusion about common abbreviations. While FYI (For Your Information) and BTW (By The Way) are relatively common outside of email, there are a number of abbreviations that aren't seen often except in email:

- IMHO - In My Humble Opinion
- RTFM - Read The Manual
- LOL - [I] Laughed Out Loud
- ROTFL - [I am] Rolling On The Floor Laughing
- RSN - Real Soon Now
- TIA - Thanks In Advance
- YMMV - Your Mileage May Vary (meaning "your experiences might be different")
- <g> - grin

In addition, every company has its own acronyms and code names. For example, Intel Corporation uses NCG to mean "New College Graduate." NASA has so many acronyms that its employees joke that it stands for "National Acronym-Slinging Agency."

Alas, frequently someone will send a message to a huge mailing list asking questions like, "What does IMHO mean?" If there are 500 people on the mailing list, the message will probably annoy 450 of them.

To let everyone know what these words and abbreviations mean, your company might want to have a Web page with a list of the signal words, abbreviations, and code words that your company uses. Even if someone explains the signal words and abbreviations once to every employee, there can still be trouble in the future. People will forget, new situations will call for new signal words, and new people will join the company.

The new hire orientation should impress upon people that if they don't understand a phrase, they should *not* ask everybody on a mailing list. Tell them to ask either the sender of the message or the person responsible for the acronyms Web page.

Signatures

Different companies have different attitudes towards signatures. It can be worthwhile to discuss signatures at new-hire orientation. Even if there isn't a company policy, it would be good for people to understand the issues surrounding signatures.

Some people like to see signatures with the name, phone number, and/or position in the company for internal mail. Others prefer to receive uncluttered messages. They figure that if they want a colleague's contact information, they can look it up in the company directory. Some corporate cultures allow humorous sayings in the signature. This can be fun. It can also look unprofessional.

For external mail, your company might want to ask people to include lots of information in a text signature. People outside the company probably can't see your company directory.

Priority Levels

Priority levels can be very useful—if everyone knows what the priority means. Unfortunately, left to their own devices, people will use radically different priorities for the same circumstances. Some will never set a priority and others will make everything top priority. Some will set priority according to how important it is to the sender while others will set priority according to how important it is to the receiver. Thus, many readers ignore priority levels completely. (Some even use filters to change the priority level.)

Another problem is that priority is a combination of urgency and importance, but there is a big difference between the two. For example, "Do you want to go to lunch with me in an hour" is high urgency but low importance. On the other hand, "I will need a bone marrow transplant in a year. Please register to be a bone marrow donor" is high importance but low urgency.

Coming up with and training people on some company-wide guidelines for priority levels will make them more useful for everybody.

Voice Instead of Email

There are times when phone or face-to-face conversations are better than email. If the topic is emotionally charged or if there are many intertwined issues to resolve, voice is frequently better. Education is the key to getting people to use the right medium for the message.

Response Speed

Differences in response speed can cause problems. If someone who thinks that people should respond to email immediately sends email to someone who replies a week later, there could be trouble.

It is difficult to set firm policy on response time because of unintended consequences. If the boss orders that everyone must respond within a certain amount of time, people will probably set up their filters to respond to *all* messages with "I got your message and am looking into your issue." This is not helpful.

If your company makes a policy insisting that employees must answer messages in a certain amount of time or not at all, then people might choose to never respond. This is also not helpful.

Your company might want to suggest to its employees that if they can tell it will take more than a day to find the answer to a question, that they should send a courtesy response. This response should say why they can't respond and when they expect to know enough to be able to respond.

It could be that some people have slow response time simply because they are buried in email. In that case, some training on how to manage email might be appropriate. Give them a copy of this book or get them to email management training. If they still can't cope with the flood of messages, perhaps they need email management software (as described on page 221) or an assistant to help them deal with all the messages.

Write Email Well

Writing clear messages can reduce the number of responses that people send. If quotes are not an appropriate length, if lines aren't wrapped well, if messages are too long, or if they cover too many topics, it will take longer to finish the conversation.

It is difficult to order people to write messages well because people almost never *try* to write poorly. Training, however, can be useful. Give everybody a copy of this book, send them to a class, or develop a Web page with hints, tips, and links to resources for writing well.

Emoticons

Some people really hate emoticons, despite how helpful they can be in conveying emotional tone properly. Some language purists find emoticons to be an assault on proper usage. Some people think emoticons are unprofessional. Other people use text-to-speech processors, which render emoticons unintelligible or invisible.

Your company might want to make sure that everyone understands the reasons for emoticons as well as their limitations.

Set Policy

One way to change behavior is to put it into the company policy. The benefits of doing things by decree are that it can be efficient and costs very little directly. The bad news is that the indirect costs can be high if people don't like the policy: grumbling and unhappiness can hurt productivity. Furthermore, there are always gray areas: behaviors that decrees can't cover or that can't be enforced. For example, "write better messages" is not a meaningful order. People don't usually write poorly on purpose.

Email is a new enough medium for most companies that sometimes it isn't clear who is responsible for making high-level decisions about email. Even if you aren't part of the management chain, you might be able to affect your company's email culture by asking the senior management, "Who is responsible for email policy decisions?" Getting an answer to that question means that somebody now has ownership of the problem. This, by itself, might be a big enough step to lead to changes.

Each company's management will have differing abilities to dictate policy, depending upon the company's overall culture. The military can tell people what to do much more easily than a charity staffed by volunteers.

That said, there are times when management needs to set policies about email usage. Management should make policies clear for any issues with legal implications, as in the following examples.

Personal Use

If your company does not have a policy against it, people will use email for their personal use. This can be good. People might not need to leave work if they can take care of errands by email. Email is also quieter than talking on the telephone—which people who work in high-density offices will appreciate.

Personal use can also hurt productivity. People can end up spending a lot of time on personal email. Jokes, hoaxes, and chain letters can be a particularly wasteful.

However, limiting employees' email access can make them resentful, especially if other companies in your area allow it. Limiting email access might limit your ability to attract and retain employees.

Your company probably needs to have a policy on acceptable behavior, which could include a recommendation that employees use a separate account for personal messages.

Illegal Uses

Many things are just as illegal on-line as they are off-line. Depending upon your jurisdiction, the following can be illegal: harassment, stalking, libel, fraud, gambling, and pyramid schemes. Your company should have a clear policy stating that your company will not tolerate illegal uses of email. Be sure to give clear examples of unacceptable behavior.

Privacy

Depending upon your jurisdiction, your company might have the legal right to examine employees' email. There are some situations where clearly it makes sense for a company to exercise that right. For example, system administrators sometimes need to glance at someone's email to make sure that they fixed a problem with the email system properly.

However, employees will probably get upset if someone reads their messages for no obvious reason. Your company might want to say who can read email under what circumstances. For example, the policy could say that reading someone else's email is cause for disciplinary action except when:

- fixing a problem in the email system
- developing a defense for a legal case
- providing subpoenaed material
- investigating illegal activities (including theft of intellectual property)
- authorized by a vice president

The company's email privacy policy should be stated clearly, perhaps at orientation or in the personnel policy.

Addresses

One thing that is definitely a policy issue is assignment of email addresses. Does your company allow people to choose any address that they like? Or does it insist on a formulaic address, like "first initial-last name"? People might want to choose their own email addresses, but others might have a better chance of finding addresses if your company uses a set formula. On the other hand, a formula might cause people to send email to the wrong place. For example, if a second lee shows up, the first lee might frequently get the second lee's email. If everyone has an unusual email address, people have an incentive to look it up.

Another issue is public visibility of email addresses. If everyone has a formulaic address, then it's easy for outsiders to guess email addresses. This can be good (customers who lose an employee's business card can still find him or her) and bad (recruiters from other companies can send email to your employees).

Your company might choose to assign you two different email addresses: the formulaic one to give to outside people and a user-selected address to give to inside people. Which address someone uses will show where the email came from and make it easier to filter.

Your company might formally recommend that employees use a different email address for any public correspondence (like Usenet newsgroups).

Attachments

What formats are okay to send as attachments? If a minority isn't able to view attachments in a certain format, what is the policy? Is the minority obliged to find software that can read it or is the majority obliged to find a format that everybody can read?

One way to address this issue is to have a list of approved formats and to issue a policy directive that everyone must have the appropriate software loaded on their computer. Another approach is to say that the person requesting the favor bears the burden of translating the document into a usable format.

It is also helpful to set limits on the size of attachments people can send. Attachments can be very large, and if the attachment goes to 500 people, that's 500 disk drives that the attachment takes space on. Instead, your company might want people to put large documents on a file server or Web server.

People Who Circumvent Technology Channels

If your company has technically-savvy employees, they might be able to set up their own email servers and/or Internet connections. Sometimes there might be good reasons for doing this. For example, if someone is developing new email list software, they will have to set up their own list servers.

However, these unofficial servers can sometimes bypass important security features. Your company might want to state that setting up an email server without the prior written permission of the Information Technology department is grounds for disciplinary action.

Email vs. Telephone

Some people don't like email. I know people who don't read their email because "if it's important, they'll telephone." This eliminates many of the benefits of email.

Frequently this culture clash forms along age, gender, and job position. While many older workers are quite comfortable with email, the minority of people who are not comfortable with email tend to be older. Older men, particularly, don't always type well because typing used to be "woman's work" and low-status. The human-contact people—sales, marketing, human resources, and so on—also tend to like the telephone more than engineers do. Engineers tend to be more comfortable with email than non-technical people are.

Given that senior management tends to be older men with non-technical backgrounds, there can be more email resistance as you move up the management chain. This can make it difficult to change policy. The senior executives might find it a loss of face to admit difficulty with email, so they might not be receptive to training or persuasion, either.

The best way to get people to read their email is to make it part of everyone's performance evaluation: does the employee respond promptly to requests from others? If email messages are a significant part of your corporate communication, your company might also want to ask all job applicants how comfortable they are with email.

Summary

Developing resources, providing training, and setting policy are all ways of improving an company's email productivity. Useful resources include:

- Web-based applications to archive mailing lists, communicate with list servers, indicate where someone has gone configure out-of-office auto-responses, and discuss corporate announcements
- Web-based applications Web-based applications for
  - software to monitor outgoing messages for confidential information
  - software to eliminate duplicate messages
  - software to remove viruses
  - for messages about food, car lights left on, items for sale, and recommendations
- a good Web site
- pre-written responses
- pre-written filters

Training can improve understanding of:

- abbreviations and signal words
- signatures
- when to use voice instead of email transactions
- appropriate response times
- when to use `Bcc:`
- how to write clearer email messages
- when to use emoticons

Management should clarify what is expected regarding:

- personal use of email
- illegal uses
- privacy
- email addresses
- attachments
- setting up alternate email servers
- reading email

Glossary

This glossary cannot be an ultimate authority. Electronic mail is still relatively new, and the language has not completely settled down yet. For example, *newsgroups*, *discussion groups*, and *electronic forums* are all the same thing—many-to-many textual conversations that can happen over long periods of time—but they have different names depending upon who is talking about them. Words also take on multiple meanings because there aren't other good terms. For example, *a client* can be a piece of hardware, a piece of software, or the combination of the two. You can sometimes figure it out from context, but not always. Use this glossary as a guide only.

account
Usually used as a synonym for email address or login ID. (Billing accounts are frequently identified by login IDs.)

action
A sequence of manipulations that a filter performs on all messages that match the given conditions.

address
A unique identifier used to determine where to send someone's email. Usually made up of the login ID, the at sign (@), and the name of the company or Internet Service Provider.

advTHANKSance
A cute way of saying *Thanks In Advance*.

AFAIK
Abbreviation for *As Far As I Know*.

alias
Same as *nickname*.

article	Message sent to many people. Usenet term; not frequently used to refer to an email message.
BCC	BCC is an abbreviation for *Blind Carbon Copy.* "Blind" indicates that the receivers can't see who is on the `Bcc:` list. See also *CC.*
body	The part of a message that contains the conversation — as opposed to the part that has information *about* the message like the time and date, sender, transmission path, and so on. See also *header.*
bounce	To be returned as undeliverable. "I tried to send you the summer picnic menu, but the message bounced." Also sometimes used as a noun to refer to a bounced message.
BTW	Abbreviation for *By The Way.* "BTW, I loved the curried mushrooms and broccoli appetizer!"
burst	To split a mailing list digest into individual messages.
CC	CC is an abbreviation for *Carbon Copy* and comes from the days when people had to use carbon paper to make copies.
	For those of you who are too young to remember, *carbon paper* used to be one of the only ways to duplicate a document. To make a copy, one had to place a sheet of carbon paper between two pieces of regular paper. Pressure from writing or typing on the top paper would transfer through the carbon paper and leave marks on the bottom paper. While people now rarely use carbon paper for duplicating documents, you can still occasionally see carbon paper in credit card signature slips.
chat	A real-time textual conversation, often with many participants.

client	A program that depends upon a program that is running on a different computer. There are now many services available where one program runs on one computer, another runs on a different computer, and they communicate over a network. The program that provides the service is called the *server* and the program that uses the service is called the *client*. (The language is a bit imprecise; the respective computers are also frequently called servers and clients.)
	One good example of a client-server application is the Web. A Web *client* or *browser* runs on an individual's personal computer. The browser connects to a Web *server*, which gives the client the Web page for display. Email is also a client-server application. Messages come to a mailbox on a mail *server*, where they stay until a mail *client* retrieves them.
condition	The piece of the filter that determines whether or not the email software will execute the specified action. Also called *criteria* by some email programs.
criteria	Same as *conditions* in filters.
CRM	Abbreviation for *Customer Relationship Management* [software].
Customer Relationship Management	A type of software that tracks interactions with customers, makes using a shared database of knowledge easier, and directs questions to the most appropriate person.
digest	A collection of messages to a mailing list that are packaged together and sent as one message.
discussion group	For practical purposes, same as *newsgroup*.
distribution list	Same as *mailing list*.

eCRM	Abbreviation for *Electronic Customer Relationship Management* [software]. See *Customer Relationship Management*.
email client	A more specific and technical term for a program (like Eudora) that you use to read, organize, send, and store email messages. See also *client*.
email ID	Same as *login ID*.
emoticon	Cartoon faces "drawn" with text and used to express emotion. Short for "emotional icon."
ESP	Abbreviation for *Eudora Sharing Protocol*.
Eudora Sharing Protocol	A feature of Eudora that lets you synchronize files over email.
envelope information	Also called a message *header*. See *header*.
EOM	Abbreviation for *End Of Message*.
FCC	Abbreviation for *File Carbon Copy*. FCC'd messages are copied to a mailbox. See also *CC*.
filter	Filters are tools in an email program that automatically take actions based upon the contents of a message and rules that you define.
	Note that *email filters* are different from *web filters*. Web filters are a form of censorship, designed to prevent people from viewing certain web pages. Web filters might have many different conditions but have only one action: disallow viewing the page. Email filters usually have many possible conditions but also several possible actions. And while web filtering software is designed so that the person browsing the Web can't modify the filters, email filters usually are under the control of the person reading the messages.

flame	An angry or insulting message. "I sent a warning to everyone in the company about the Good Times virus, and fifty people flamed me for wasting resources!"
flame war	A series of angry or insulting messages between two or more correspondents.
folder	As used by Eudora, a collection of mailboxes. Caution: many other email programs use the term *folder* where Eudora uses the term *mailbox*.
forum	For practical purposes, same as *newsgroup*.
forward	To send a copy of a message to a third party. "I hope you don't mind, but your essay about learning how to drive was so funny that I forwarded it to my Aunt Sonia."
FUMLUB	Eudora-specific abbreviation meaning *First Unread Message of Last Unread Batch*.
FWIW	Abbreviation for *For What It's Worth*. "I know you're concerned about shaving your head, but FWIW, nobody has ever hassled me about my shaved head."
FYI	Abbreviation for *For Your Information*. "FYI—someone stole Fred's bicycle this morning, so he's in a bad mood."
GMTA	Abbreviation for *Great Minds Think Alike*.
header	A piece of information *about* an email message. Headers typically show who sent the message, who it was addressed to, the date and time that it was sent, and some information about the path that the message took. *Header* can refer to either the entire set of information or to just one piece (such as the subject or the date). Also called *envelope information*.
HTML	Abbreviation for *HyperText Markup Language*. See *HyperText Markup Language*.

hyperlink	Text that, when clicked upon, initiates an action (like retrieving a Web page).
HyperText Markup Language	The language used to create most Web pages.
IETF	Abbreviation for *Internet Engineering Task Force*. See *Internet Engineering Task Force*.
IHAC	Abbreviation for *I Have A Customer*. "IHAC who says that he broke the cup-holder on his computer."
IMAP	Abbreviation for *Internet Messaging Access Protocol*. See *Internet Messaging Access Protocol*.
IMHO	Abbreviation for *In My Humble Opinion* or *In My Honest Opinion*. "IMHO, Eudora is the best email program available."
IMNSHO	Abbreviation for *In My Not-So-Humble Opinion*.
intranet	A set of computers that communicate with each other with TCP/IP, can access machines on the Internet, but that can only be accessed by computers that are on the same local network. Machines on an intranet are not supposed to be publicly accessible.
Internet	When capitalized, it refers to a specific extremely large network of computers that communicate with each other using the TCP/IP specifications and that are publicly accessible. When not capitalized, refers to a network of computers connected by a TCP/IP network that are *not* attached to the public network.
Internet Messaging Access Protocol	A type of server-based email system. Messages are kept on a server and only temporarily stored on the client. (This is different from *Post Office Protocol* (POP), where messages are stored on the client and only temporarily stored on the server.)

In practical terms, IMAP lets you access your email from two or more computers and it will always look the same. The disadvantage of IMAP is that you need to stay connected to the Internet for the whole time you are working with your email.

With POP, the messages are stored on the computer you used to read them. If you go to another computer, you won't see all the messages because some or all are on the first computer. See also *Post Office Protocol*.

Internet Engineering Task Force	A group that develops standards for Internet technologies, including email.
Internet Service Provider	An organization that provides access to the Internet. If you get your email through your company, then your company is your Internet Service Provider.
ISP	Abbreviation for *Internet Service Provider*. See *Internet Service Provider*.
Light mode	A version of Eudora 5 that is free, but with fewer features than Paid mode or Sponsored mode.
listbot	Although the name of a particular list server site, this term is frequently used as a generic synonym for *list server*.
listname address	The email address that reaches all the subscribers on a mailing list. This is *not* the same as the list server address, which is used for communicating with the list server software.
listserv	The name of an early *list server* software package. Some people now use it to mean a list server *or* mailing list.
list server	A program that automatically administers a mailing list. "If you don't want to get any more messages, don't tell the list, send an unsubscribe message to the list server." Also called a *listserv* or *listbot*.

list server address	Email address used to communicate with list server software.
live text	See *hyperlink*.
login ID	The unique identifier used for signing on to a computer or email account. Same as *handle, username, email ID*, and (sometimes) *account*.
LOL	Abbreviation for *Laughing Out Loud*.
lurker	A person who reads messages on a mailing list or Usenet newsgroup but does not write (post) any messages.
mailbox	A collection of messages.
mailing list	A free-flowing, many-to-many email conversation with shifting membership. A piece of software (called a *list server, listbot*, or *listserv*) will take any messages to a particular email address and re-send them to everybody who has subscribed to that list. Also called *distribution list*.
Mail Transport Agent	A very technical term for the software that takes a message and transmits it to the destination computer.
Mail User Agent	A very technical term for the email software that a user interacts with. Same as *email client*.
majordomo	The name of a very widely-used *list server*.
Message-ID	The message header that gives a unique identifier to each message.
MIME	Abbreviation for *Multipart Internet Mail Extensions*, an extension to the original email specifications that allows sending messages in essentially any format. (It does not, however, guarantee that the receiver's computer will be able to display any format.)

MLM	Abbreviation for *Multi-Level Marketing*. See *Multi-Level Marketing*.
MTA	Abbreviation for *Mail Transport Agent*. See *Mail Transport Agent*.
MUA	Abbreviation for *Mail User Agent*. See *Mail User Agent*.
Multi-Level Marketing	A type of *pyramid scheme*.
newbie	A person who is new to the Internet. Depending upon how it is used, it can be derogatory.
newsgroup	A forum where many people can read and write (post) messages. Once this word only referred to Usenet discussions, but now the word is drifting to include Web-based discussions. "One of the basketball newsgroups had a posting that someone is going to start a second women's professional league."
nickname	A shortcut for either a single email address or a group of email addresses. For example, you might have a group nickname roses that contains the email addresses of seven people in your rose gardening club. Then if you addressed a message to roses, your email software would send the message to those seven club members. Also called *alias, group,* or *card.*
NRN	Abbreviation for *No Reply Needed*. This is not common, but I would like to see it become common.
off-topic	About something that is not directly related to a mailing list's stated purpose.
OT	Common (but by no means universal) abbreviation for *Off-Topic.*

OTOH	Abbreviation for *On The Other Hand.* "I think the U. S. president is incompetent. OTOH, her husband is the best politician I've ever seen."
outbox	A mailbox containing copies of messages that have been sent. "I looked through my outbox for my last message to him, and I sent him the report last Thursday."
Paid mode	A version of Eudora 5 that has all the features and no advertising. See also *Sponsored mode* and *Light mode.*
Ponzi scheme	A particular type of *pyramid scheme.*
POP	Abbreviation for *Post Office Protocol.* See *Post Office Protocol.*
Post Office Protocol	One specification for how computers must talk to each other to transfer a message from an email server to an email client. Post Office Protocol (commonly abbreviated POP) systems are designed for the user to download, store, and manipulate mail on the user's desktop machine. This is different from IMAP, where the mail is stored and manipulated on a server.
post	To write a message for a large group. One implication of *post* instead of *write* is that the message will be public and not private. "Somebody posted to the Stanford alumni mailing list that they had a job vacancy to fill in floss recycling."
protocol	A set of rules that computers use to talk to each other. There are many protocols for many purposes, including sending email, transferring email, and sending instant messages.
pyramid scheme	A scheme where later participants (B) pay money to earlier participants (A) in the hope that even later participants (C) will give them (B) even larger sums of money than they (B) gave to earlier participants (A). This is almost

always illegal (except when investing in stock market bubbles).

redirect To forward in a manner where the message appears to come directly from the original author, not the person who forwarded it.

regexp A way of compactly describing a set of similar text strings. Also known as *regular expression*.

Reply-to-All The method of replying where every person in the `From:`, `To:` and `Cc:` headers get the response, not just the person on the `From:` line. See also Reply-to-Sender.

Reply-to-Sender The method of replying where only the person in the `From:` header gets the response, not also any people in the `To:` and `Cc:` headers. See also Reply-to-All.

RFC Abbreviation for *Request For Comments*, but almost nobody uses the long form. Originally, RFCs *were* requests for comments. In practice, now RFCs are the rules for how computers talk to each other over the Internet.

RFC822 RFC822 is the name of the original specification for email—before rich text, attachments, and many of the other features of modern email. To say that a message is "RFC822", then, is to say that its formatting is very simple.

ROTFL Abbreviation for *Rolling On The Floor Laughing*.

ROTFLMAO Abbreviation for *Rolling On The Floor Laughing* (ahem) *hard*.

router A specialized computer that is responsible for sending information onwards towards its final destination.

RSN	Abbreviation for *Real Soon Now*. This is usually used jokingly when something has been promised (and delayed) for a long time. If you read RSN, you should probably not believe that the item under discussion is going to be ready any time soon.
RTFM	Abbreviation for *Read The* (ahem) *Manual*.
rule	Microsoft's term for *filter*.
screen name	One of many email IDs associated with one billing account.
sendmail	Sendmail is the most common *Mail Transport Agent*. Sendmail takes a message and sends it on towards its final destination. See also Mail Transport Agent.
server	Software and/or hardware that provides a service (like Web pages) over a network. See also *client*.
Simple Mail Transport Protocol	The protocol (rules) that computers use to talk to each other to send email towards its destination.
snailmail	Techno-slang for postal (paper) mail.
smiley	Same as *emoticon*.
SMTP	Abbreviation for *Simple Mail Transport Protocol*. See *Simple Mail Transport Protocol*.
Sponsored mode	A version of Eudora 5 that has all the features of Paid mode, but shows you advertisements. See also *Paid mode* and *Light mode*.
subscribe	To join [a mailing list].

spam	Techno-slang for *Unsolicited Commercial Email.* It apparently comes from an episode of the Monty Python television show, and is not usually capitalized except at the beginning of sentences. (The words *Spam* and *SPAM* are brand names for a particular brand of canned meat.)
TCP/IP	Abbreviation for *Transmission Control Protocol/Internet Protocol,* but almost nobody uses the long form. TCP/IP refers to the set of rules that computers on the Internet use to talk to each other.
thread	A thread is a set of messages on the same topic. Threads usually have the same `Subject:` or have information in the header that connects a message with the previous message.
TIA	Abbreviation for *Thanks In Advance.*
UCE	Abbreviation for *Unsolicited Commercial Email.*
Uniform Resource Locator	A Web address, for example `http://www.webfoot.com`.
Unsolicited Commercial Email	Fancy name for junk email.
unsubscribe	To request to be removed [from a mailing list].
URL	Abbreviation for *Uniform Resource Locator.* See *Uniform Resource Locator.*
Usenet	An application that lets many people write (or *post*) and read messages (or *articles*). Articles are distributed by copying them from computer to computer. Usenet is the original Internet discussion forum, but there are now many types.
username	Same as *login ID.*

viral marketing	Viral marketing is a term for any product that encourages (or forces) its customers to advertise the product. For example, many free email services include a mini-ad for their service at the bottom of each message that is sent via the service. This book is another example: if you want to get more readable email, you should convince your correspondents to also read this book.
word-wrap	What happens with text where the width of the screen is smaller than the number of characters until a carriage return. If the text is broken into lines at word boundaries, it is word-wrapped. If the text is not broken into lines or is broken in the middle of words, it is not word-wrapped.
YMMV	Abbreviation for *Your Mileage May Vary*, a standard disclaimer in automobile advertisements in the United States. It means, basically, that the author believes his or her statement to be true but recognizes that it might not be a universal truth. "I've never had trouble buying a ticket right before the show starts, but YMMV."

Mailboxes and Labels

This appendix explains how to do a few things that are pretty simple, but that you might not have seen. It explains how to create collections of messages (mailboxes) and collections of collections (folders) and how to configure labels.

Mailboxes

Mailboxes are collections of messages. Your inbox is one example of a mailbox. Mailboxes are very useful for organizing and prioritizing your messages.

To create a mailbox, select Mailbox →*New…* and a window like one in Figure 39 will appear:

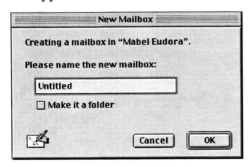

Figure 39: New Mailbox Window (Mac OS and Windows)

Type in the name of the new mailbox and click OK.

To delete a mailbox, first open the mailboxes window as explained above. Select the mailbox you want to remove and press the `delete` key.

Folders

You can also group mailboxes together in folders. To create a new folder with menus, select `Mailbox` →*New...* as above. To make a folder, put a checkmark in the box labeled `Make this a folder` and type in the name you want the folder to have.

Labels

With Eudora, you can categorize a message by giving it what Eudora calls a *label*. Labels let you attach a category, a color, and even a priority to a message.

To configure labels, select `Special`→`Settings...`→`Labels` (Mac OS) or `Tools`→`Options...`→`Labels` (Windows).

You can change the color and name of labels, as shown in Figure 40 (Windows) and Figure 41 (Mac OS):

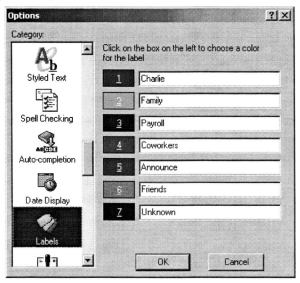

Figure 40: Eudora Labels (Windows)

To change the color, click on one of the boxes on the left. To change the name of the label, enter the new name on the right.

If you are using Windows, you can use seven labels. Eudora for Mac OS has eight Eudora labels, but you can also use the seven operating system labels for a total of fifteen.

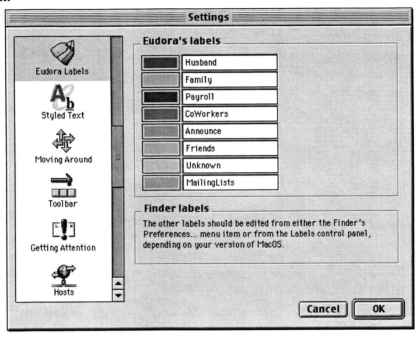

Figure 41: Eudora labels settings (Mac OS)

To edit the system labels with Mac OS 9, go to the Finder and select Edit→Preferences…→Labels.

You can use colors to give you clues to a message's priority. Bright red, green, and blue all stand out very well on computer monitors, so you should use those colors for important messages. You should use pale colors or ones that don't have a clear contrast with the white background (like yellow or grey) for low-priority messages.

When looking at a mailbox, the text of the entry for a message is the color of its label. This makes it very easy to tell what category a message belongs to. For example, if the Charlie label is red, then the first two lines in the mailbox shown in Figure 42 will be red:

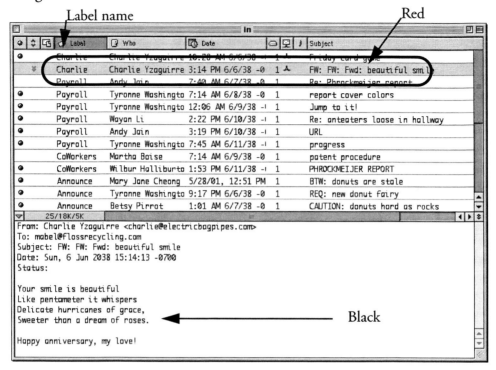

Figure 42: Label Text and Color

The color of message body text is not affected by the label color. If the message is open in its own window, however, the top of the window has a horizontal bar in the same color as the label, as seen in Figure 43.

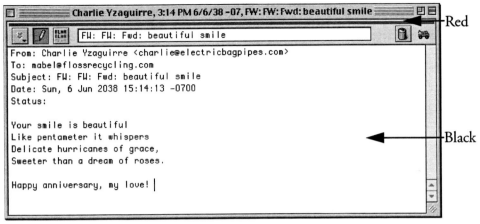

Figure 43: Bar in Label Color (Mac OS)

Summary

- To create a new mailbox, click on the "new mailbox" button in the Mailboxes window or select the menu item Mailbox→New….
- To create a new folder, do the same thing you'd do to create a mailbox, but put a checkmark in the box next to Make this a folder.
- To edit the Eudora labels, select Special→Settings…→Labels (Mac OS) or Tools→Options…→Labels (Windows) window.
- Eudora for Windows lets you use up to seven labels. Eudora for Mac OS lets you use up to eight Eudora labels and seven Mac OS labels.
- In a mailbox view, you can see what labels messages have by looking at the Label column and the color of the message entry text.
- Body text color is unaffected by label color.
- If a message is in its own window, you can see what label it has by looking at the color of the horizontal line at the top of the message.

Index

Symbols

*, emphasizing with 168
<> around URLs 184

A

actions, filter
  about 36
  advanced 49
  make label 39
  make priority 50
  mark importance 50
  open message/mailbox 49
  play sound 51
addressee list, suppressing 123, 125
addresses, policy 231
addressing methods
  responding to 138
  signaling importance with 197
  see also Bcc, Cc, and To
advTHANKSance visual pun 120
alerts, disabling 53
ambiguity
  intonational grouping 165
  of common names 158
  of concepts 159
  of place 159
  of references 157–161
  of time 160
  reducing with emphasis 167
archiving messages, benefits of 98
asterisks 168
attachments
  about 178

incompatibilities 187
policy 232
audience, intended 20
auto-responders
  dangers of 150
  for blocking strangers 150
  loops 152, 153
  out-of-office messages 151
  web interface to 223

B

backwards compatibility 23
Bcc:
  about 123
  dangers of 123
  for reducing further traffic 123
  origin of term 236
  responding to 138
  signaling unimportance with 199
blacklist 82
BLAH BLAH BLAH button 26, 178
buttons
  adding to toolbar 95–98
  BLAH BLAH BLAH button 26, 178
  pencil button 191
  strip formatting button 181

C

capital letters, using 173
categories
  humor 33
  one per mailing list 33
  organizing
    by project 32
    by sender 32

suppressing addressee list 123, 125, 202

T

telephone vs. email 176, 232
templates, see stationery
terminology, about 24
testing filters 56
text-to-speech processors 170
thank you 119, 136
TIA 120
time, see ambiguity, in time
To: header, signaling importance with 197
to-do items
   hiding finished messages 47
   organizing by label 47
   organizing by mailbox 48
toolbar, modifying 95–98
training 224

U

um and uh 173
uncertainty, expressing 172
unsubscribing
   how to 112
   how not to 114
unwrapping text 190
uppercase letters, using 173
urgency 173
URLs 183–186

V

vacation messages
   see auto-responders,
   see out-of-office messages
versions, see Eudora versions

viruses
   chain letters 129
   hoaxes 130
   preventing 188
   virus-checkers 219
visual aids 23
visually impaired correspondents 170
voice vs. email, see speech vs. email
voting 129

W

ways to look stupid 114, 124, 127, 130, 133, 137, 140, 152, 156, 159, 204
whitespace, in HTML messages 182
windows
   customize toolbar 97
   Filter Window 37
   making smaller 105
word unwrapping, see unwrapping text
word wrapping 189
writing, nonstandard 174

Y

you're welcome 119, 136

About the Author

Kaitlin Duck Sherwood worked in a cornfield, fast-food restaurant, space suit design lab, semiconductor manufacturing factory, university, and three bankrupt high-tech startups before venturing out into her own. She worked as a software consultant for four lucrative but boring years before going back to graduate school—where she discovered the World Wide Web. Her Web-based projects earned her two awards and an outstanding case of repetitive strain injury. She worked as a Smalltalk programmer for two years years after she (mostly) recovered and before starting this book project.

Sherwood has been using electronic mail since 1973 and Internet email since 1985. In 1994, she developed what might have been the very first Web-based email system.

Sherwood's Web site gets over 100,000 hits per month, with most visitors going to her tutorial, *A Beginner's Guide to Effective Email.*

Quick Tips for Overcoming Email Overload

1. **If your email program has tools called *rules* or *filters*, use them to automatically prioritize your inbox.** If possible, use rules to assign each message a category (or *label*) based on what group the sender belongs to. If you assign the categories so that they sort in the same order as their probable importance, then you can easily sort your inbox to list messages in roughly the order you want to deal with them.

2. **If your email program allows it, put buttons in the toolbar for moving the selected message(s) to a final resting place and for moving to the next message.** If you are done with a message, press the first button. If you still need to do something with a message, press the second button.

3. **Use filters/rules to assign junk email a very low-priority category or move it to another mailbox.** (But do not delete junk email automatically! Your rules will make mistakes sometimes.)

4. **Unsubscribe from as many mailing lists as you can.**

5. **Get and use a free email account for all transactions with retailers or the public.**

6. **Use formal language and end messages with "No Reply Needed" to discourage responses.**

7. **As much as possible, reply to only the sender instead of to everybody and use BCC instead of CC.**

8. **Don't forward any message that asks you to forward it to everyone you know.** Those messages are almost always hoaxes or out of date. You might get lots of messages back telling you so.

9. **If someone sends you messages you don't want (like hoaxes or jokes), ask them (*very* politely) to stop.** Otherwise, they will send you more.

10. **Be sure to provide adequate context for your messages.** Quote previous messages carefully and watch for references to people or things that you don't mention in the message.

11. **Save and reuse responses to questions that you get frequently.**

12. **Make your emotional tone as obvious and explicit as you can.**

13. **Use styled text infrequently.** If your messages are too pretty, people might think you don't have enough to do.

14. **Discuss only one issue per message.** People frequently forget about all but the first or last question.

15. **Visit** `http://www.OvercomeEmailOverload.com` **for more resources.**

16. **Buy and read a book in the *Overcome Email Overload* series** (see reverse).

Help your friends overcome email overload: give them this page!

Postal orders: PO Box 36, Palo Alto, CA 94302-0036 USA. Make checks payable to World Wide Webfoot Press.
Paypal orders: *bookorder@webfoot.com*
Web orders: http://www.OvercomeEmailOverload.com/orderForm.html
Phone and fax orders: see the Web site for the latest information

Please send the following with your orders:

Item	Price	Qty.	Total
Overcome Email Overload with Microsoft Outlook 2000 and Outlook 2002	US$29.95		
Overcome Email Overload with Eudora 5	US$29.95		
postage for first book (US)	US$5.00		
postage for additional books (US)	US$2.00		
postage per book (Canada and Mexico)	US$7.00		
postage per book (all other countries)	US$9.00		
tax per book (California only)	US$2.40		
information about training and consulting	Free!		$0.00
Total			

TO: Name: _____

        Address: _____

        City: _____

        ZIP or Postal Code: _____   Country: _____

Credit card (circle one): Visa MasterCard   **Name on Card:** _____

Account number: _____   **Expiration date:** ___/____

Quick Tips for Overcoming Email Overload

1. If your email program has tools called *rules* or *filters*, use them to automatically prioritize your inbox. If possible, use rules to assign each message a category (or *label*) based on what group the sender belongs to. If you assign the categories so that they sort in the same order as their probable importance, then you can easily sort your inbox to list messages in roughly the order you want to deal with them.

2. If your email program allows it, put buttons in the toolbar for moving the selected message(s) to a final resting place and for moving to the next message. If you are done with a message, press the first button. If you still need to do something with a message, press the second button.

3. Use filters/rules to assign junk email a very low-priority category or move it to another mailbox. (But do not delete junk email automatically! Your rules will make mistakes sometimes.)

4. Unsubscribe from as many mailing lists as you can.

5. Get and use a free email account for all transactions with retailers or the public.

6. Use formal language and end messages with "No Reply Needed" to discourage responses.

7. As much as possible, reply to only the sender instead of to everybody and use BCC instead of CC.

8. Don't forward any message that asks you to forward it to everyone you know. Those messages are almost always hoaxes or out of date. You might get lots of messages back telling you so.

9. If someone sends you messages you don't want (like hoaxes or jokes), ask them (*very* politely) to stop. Otherwise, they will send you more.

10. Be sure to provide adequate context for your messages. Quote previous messages carefully and watch for references to people or things that you don't mention in the message.

11. Save and reuse responses to questions that you get frequently.

12. Make your emotional tone as obvious and explicit as you can.

13. Use styled text infrequently. If your messages are too pretty, people might think you don't have enough to do.

14. Discuss only one issue per message. People frequently forget about all but the first or last question.

15. Visit `http://www.OvercomeEmailOverload.com` for more resources.

16. Buy and read a book in the *Overcome Email Overload* series (see reverse).

Help your friends overcome email overload: give them this page!

Postal orders: PO Box 36, Palo Alto, CA 94302-0036 USA. Make checks payable to World Wide Webfoot Press.
Paypal orders: *bookorder@webfoot.com*
Web orders: `http://www.OvercomeEmailOverload.com/orderForm.html`
Phone and fax orders: see the Web site for the latest information

Please send the following with your orders:

Item	Price	Qty.	Total
Overcome Email Overload with Microsoft Outlook 2000 and Outlook 2002	US$29.95		
Overcome Email Overload with Eudora 5	US$29.95		
postage for first book (US)	US$5.00		
postage for additional books (US)	US$2.00		
postage per book (Canada and Mexico)	US$7.00		
postage per book (all other countries)	US$9.00		
tax per book (California only)	US$2.40		
information about training and consulting	Free!		$0.00
Total			

TO: Name: _____

      Address: _____

      City: _____

      ZIP or Postal Code: _____   Country: _____

Credit card (circle one): Visa MasterCard **Name on Card:** _____

Account number: _____   **Expiration date:** ___/____

Quick Tips for Overcoming Email Overload

1. **If your email program has tools called *rules* or *filters*, use them to automatically prioritize your inbox.** If possible, use rules to assign each message a category (or *label*) based on what group the sender belongs to. If you assign the categories so that they sort in the same order as their probable importance, then you can easily sort your inbox to list messages in roughly the order you want to deal with them.

2. **If your email program allows it, put buttons in the toolbar for moving the selected message(s) to a final resting place and for moving to the next message.** If you are done with a message, press the first button. If you still need to do something with a message, press the second button.

3. **Use filters/rules to assign junk email a very low-priority category or move it to another mailbox.** (But do not delete junk email automatically! Your rules will make mistakes sometimes.)

4. **Unsubscribe from as many mailing lists as you can.**

5. **Get and use a free email account for all transactions with retailers or the public.**

6. **Use formal language and end messages with "No Reply Needed" to discourage responses.**

7. **As much as possible, reply to only the sender instead of to everybody and use BCC instead of CC.**

8. **Don't forward any message that asks you to forward it to everyone you know.** Those messages are almost always hoaxes or out of date. You might get lots of messages back telling you so.

9. **If someone sends you messages you don't want (like hoaxes or jokes), ask them (*very* politely) to stop.** Otherwise, they will send you more.

10. **Be sure to provide adequate context for your messages.** Quote previous messages carefully and watch for references to people or things that you don't mention in the message.

11. **Save and reuse responses to questions that you get frequently.**

12. **Make your emotional tone as obvious and explicit as you can.**

13. **Use styled text infrequently.** If your messages are too pretty, people might think you don't have enough to do.

14. **Discuss only one issue per message.** People frequently forget about all but the first or last question.

15. **Visit** `http://www.OvercomeEmailOverload.com` **for more resources.**

16. **Buy and read a book in the *Overcome Email Overload* series** (see reverse).

Help your friends overcome email overload: give them this page!

Postal orders: PO Box 36, Palo Alto, CA 94302-0036 USA. Make checks payable to World Wide Webfoot Press.
Paypal orders: *bookorder@webfoot.com*
Web orders: http://www.OvercomeEmailOverload.com/orderForm.html
Phone and fax orders: see the Web site for the latest information

Please send the following with your orders:

Item	Price	Qty.	Total
Overcome Email Overload with Microsoft Outlook 2000 and Outlook 2002	US$29.95		
Overcome Email Overload with Eudora 5	US$29.95		
postage for first book (US)	US$5.00		
postage for additional books (US)	US$2.00		
postage per book (Canada and Mexico)	US$7.00		
postage per book (all other countries)	US$9.00		
tax per book (California only)	US$2.40		
information about training and consulting	Free!		$0.00
Total			

TO: Name: _____

Address: _____

City: _____

ZIP or Postal Code: _____   Country: _____

Credit card (circle one): Visa MasterCard **Name on Card:** _____

Account number: _____   **Expiration date:** ___/____

Quick Tips for Overcoming Email Overload

1. **If your email program has tools called *rules* or *filters*, use them to automatically prioritize your inbox.** If possible, use rules to assign each message a category (or *label*) based on what group the sender belongs to. If you assign the categories so that they sort in the same order as their probable importance, then you can easily sort your inbox to list messages in roughly the order you want to deal with them.

2. **If your email program allows it, put buttons in the toolbar for moving the selected message(s) to a final resting place and for moving to the next message.** If you are done with a message, press the first button. If you still need to do something with a message, press the second button.

3. **Use filters/rules to assign junk email a very low-priority category or move it to another mailbox.** (But do not delete junk email automatically! Your rules will make mistakes sometimes.)

4. **Unsubscribe from as many mailing lists as you can.**

5. **Get and use a free email account for all transactions with retailers or the public.**

6. **Use formal language and end messages with "No Reply Needed" to discourage responses.**

7. **As much as possible, reply to only the sender instead of to everybody and use BCC instead of CC.**

8. **Don't forward any message that asks you to forward it to everyone you know.** Those messages are almost always hoaxes or out of date. You might get lots of messages back telling you so.

9. **If someone sends you messages you don't want (like hoaxes or jokes), ask them (*very* politely) to stop.** Otherwise, they will send you more.

10. **Be sure to provide adequate context for your messages.** Quote previous messages carefully and watch for references to people or things that you don't mention in the message.

11. **Save and reuse responses to questions that you get frequently.**

12. **Make your emotional tone as obvious and explicit as you can.**

13. **Use styled text infrequently.** If your messages are too pretty, people might think you don't have enough to do.

14. **Discuss only one issue per message.** People frequently forget about all but the first or last question.

15. **Visit** `http://www.OvercomeEmailOverload.com` **for more resources.**

16. **Buy and read a book in the *Overcome Email Overload* series** (see reverse).

Help your friends overcome email overload: give them this page!

Postal orders: PO Box 36, Palo Alto, CA 94302-0036 USA. Make checks payable to World Wide Webfoot Press.
Paypal orders: *bookorder@webfoot.com*
Web orders: `http://www.OvercomeEmailOverload.com/orderForm.html`
Phone and fax orders: see the Web site for the latest information

Please send the following with your orders:

Item	Price	Qty.	Total
Overcome Email Overload with Microsoft Outlook 2000 and Outlook 2002	US$29.95		
Overcome Email Overload with Eudora 5	US$29.95		
postage for first book (US)	US$5.00		
postage for additional books (US)	US$2.00		
postage per book (Canada and Mexico)	US$7.00		
postage per book (all other countries)	US$9.00		
tax per book (California only)	US$2.40		
information about training and consulting	Free!		$0.00
Total			

TO: Name: _____

Address: _____

City: _____

ZIP or Postal Code: _____   Country: _____

Credit card (circle one): Visa MasterCard   **Name on Card:** _____

Account number: _____   **Expiration date:** ___/____